Rosemary Ellen Guiley's
Guide to the Dark Side of the
Paranormal

Rosemary Ellen Guiley's

Guide to the Dark Side of the Paranormal

2012
Viksionary Living, Inc.
New Milford, CT
www.visionaryliving.com

First Edition
First Printing, 2012

Cover art by Robert Michael Place. Used with permission.

Visionary Living, Inc.
New Milford, Connecticut
www.visionaryliving.com

Contents

Author's Note

My work in the paranormal and metaphysical fields has always embraced both the light and dark sides of experiences and phenomena. It is easy for most people to accept the good and benevolent, and much harder to come to terms with the bad and malevolent. Some even deny the existence of the dark side, perhaps in subconscious hope that they will never encounter it, or, by ignoring it, it will cease to exist.

Many of the inquiries and requests for help that I receive from people concern troubling paranormal issues and problems. The media and religions sensationalize the dark side, and so objective information is hard to find. This collection of articles is an introduction to the shadowy underbelly of the occult, a resource for the casually curious and those involved in paranormal work. I have included some of my own experiences as well. Where appropriate, I have included helpful tips for avoiding and resolving paranormal problems, and increasing protection against paranormal influences.

1

The Power of Curses

The story is a familiar one in haunting lore: an angry, wronged person gets even by laying a curse. Like an arrow in a bull's eye, the curse hits it mark, and for generations a family, place or even land suffers under a shadow of misfortune. Whatever is cursed becomes ruined, and often haunted.

Does a curse really have the power to destroy, and to create a haunting? Or is it a convenient fiction for explaining why bad things happen and hauntings exist — a bit of colorful folklore that springs up after the fact?

Cursing is indeed a real and potent power. Cursing can create all manner of havoc: bad luck, misfortune, apparitions, poltergeist disturbances, disasters, destruction — and death.

Every culture and society on this planet has appreciated the force of a curse. Curses have been used throughout human history to right wrongs, wreak vengeance and eliminate rivals of all stripes. Since ancient times, cursing has been part of a system of justice of redress and revenge. It has even been used for competitive edge.

The Greeks and Romans used curses as a part of daily life, to gain advantage in business, politics, sports and love. They wrote curses on thin lead tablets, inscribing the victim's name, the curse, magical symbols and names of various deities or spirits invoked to carry out the curse. The tablets were buried near a fresh tomb, a battlefield or a place of execution, all of which were believed to be populated by spirits of the dead en route to the underworld. The dead were believed to give a curse a big boost of power. Curse tablets also were fixed with nails and were thrown into wells, springs or rivers, also inhabited by spirits.

So important is cursing that many societies have had professional cursers. They go by many names, such as witch, sorcerer, cunning man or woman, and shaman. They possess abilities to use magical power for better or for worse. In Hawaiian magical culture, for example, certain *kahunas* have the power to issue a death prayer. They literally pray — or curse — a person to death. The death prayer is the ultimate punishment for the most serious of crimes. The cursed person becomes ill and dies.

Types of curses

Not all curses have the trappings of a Hollywood film about witches and sorcerers. We can level curses at others every day without realizing it. Other curses are leveled in spellcasting and magical ritual.

Negative prayer. Do you believe in the power of prayer to heal? The dark side of that power is the curse — a negative prayer that harms or even kills, like the *kahuna* death prayer mentioned above. Medical doctor Larry Dossey explores the dark side of praying in his book *Prayer is Good Medicine.* Dossey documents testimony from some people who say that sometimes when they pray intensely *against* someone, bad things happen to that person.

Prayer is not just asking God to do something for you. When people direct prayer, they are engaging their own power of thought and intention and projecting it into the universe to seek a certain outcome.

Ill wishing. Have you ever had bad thoughts about someone? You have indulged in a form of cursing called ill-wishing. Ill-wishing is usually the product of envy, revenge and anger. In earlier times, the ill thoughts of a person were taken quite seriously as capable of having a tangible effect. Words such as "You'll be sorry!" meant the same as a curse.

Hexes. The term "hex" comes from the German word *hexe* for "witch." A hex is a spell or bewitchment. Actually, it can be either benign and helpful, or detrimental. However, the term "hex" has become popularly associated with negative spells and curses. Merely muttering a hex, or even engaging in ill-wishing, doesn't always put a curse in motion. The projection of intense emotion, thought and will are important elements.

Blasting. This term was more common in the past, and referred to curses leveled against the fertility and well-being of people, animals and even crops – all of which could affect a person's ability to survive. Blasting causes illness, disease and blight.

Deathbed curses. Curses made by a dying person are con-sidered to be among the most powerful, and the hardest to break. The very life force of a person goes into the curse. Deathbed curses against generations of families and against entire towns and regions are famous. In the witchcraft trials in Salem, Massachusetts in 1692, innocent people were hanged. Several cursed their executioners and even the entire town of Salem in their final moments. Accused witch Sarah Good told Reverend Nicholas Noyes, who officiated at the hangings, that if he took away her life, God would give him blood to drink. Twenty-five years later, an aneurysm in his throat caused Noyes to choke to death on his own blood.

Giles Corey, who was pressed to death by sheriff George

Corwin, cursed Corwin and all of Salem. Corwin and generations of sheriffs after him all died by mysterious blood-related disorders or heart attacks. Many current residents of Salem feel that the fortunes of the town itself, which declined after the trials, were the result of many curses of the victims.

Sin curses. Even the Bible says it: the sins of the fathers will be visited upon the children, even to the third and fourth generation. Exodus 20:5 refers to the worship of false gods, but the "sins of the fathers" has acquired a broader context. Grievous crimes and transgressions, especially by a patriarch, are believed to curse an entire family, sometimes for a long time.

Other "sin curses" involve stolen objects, and violations of sacred places.

Tools used in cursing

Speaking or even thinking a curse has power, but tools are employed in cursing as well. The tool itself doesn't bring about the curse, but in some cases helps the curser to focus his internal power. In Ireland, for example, there is an old custom of using "cursing stones," a small flat stone rubbed and turned counter-clockwise (the direction that is against the natural order) while vocalizing a curse.

One of the most common tools is a poppet, a small doll

usually filled with straw or cotton, that substitutes for the victim. The poppet operates on the principle of sympathetic magic: that what is done ritually to an object is also done to the victim. Poppets are stuck with pins in appropriate places while curses are uttered.

Food items that decay serve as tools as well. For example, a potato is stuck with pins while cursing, and then buried. As the potato decays, the curse takes effect.

Similarly, curses and other spells are bound in knots that are tied in long cords or rope while the spells are cast. When the knots are untied, the curse or spell is unleashed.

Even a "gift" can be cursed. Any object can be imbued with a curse and then passed to a person.

Why do curses work?

Curses do work – but don't get paranoid about them. If every bad thought and even every intended curse played out, we would be in a great deal of chaos. The energy of a curse works with or against many other forces at play in the universe.

Skeptics argue that no magic is at play, just human fear and nature. The target fears the curse so much that he or she subconsciously fulfills it. That may be so in some cases, but sometimes victims have no knowledge of a curse, or, if they do, dismiss it. The curse works, anyway.

So what makes a curse take hold and last? Certainly, not every ill word or thought has drastic consequences. We still do not have a thorough understanding of the powers of our own consciousness. But there are several factors that likely play a significant role in cursing:

Emotional intensity. In magic, the success of a spell or any magical operation depends heavily upon the emotional intensity of the practitioner. Emotions seem to be able to lodge in the time-space fabric, where they can have an effect for a long time. Others can experience this lodged emotion. Paranormal investigators are familiar with the emotions behind many hauntings. Negative, angry and unhappy emotions seem to have more staying power than positive emotions. These factors may be why the deathbed curse is so powerful — a dying person, filled with rage, puts every last bit of strength and energy into the curse.

A skilled magician knows how to manipulate emotional intensity with focused thought and imagination, and laser-like direction of will. However, under the right circumstances, such as emotion-laden events, ordinary persons can project the right mix of energies to make a curse take effect. They may even do so without realizing it. For example, a heinous crime can generate the right emotional pitch to curse a place with a negative haunting.

Receptivity of the victim. The belief of the victim in the power of the curse may help it last. For example, if a dying man curses the family members gathered around his bedside, the fear may lodge successfully enough so that bad things do happen. Family curses can be passed down for generations before they lose power.

The beliefs of others. If a curse becomes well-known, the beliefs of outsiders may contribute to its powers. If visitors know a place is supposed to be cursed, they may feed the curse and keep it active. Interestingly, it often does not matter if the events behind a curse are real or embellished folklore. If enough people believe, the curse takes on its own real power.

Geophysical factors. When a place or land is cursed, there may be something literally in the landscape that energizes the emotional energy and keeps the curse alive. There may be some composition of rock or soil, for example, which feeds hauntings in general. Quartz, water-retentive clay and radon have been linked to hot haunting areas.

Is cursing immoral?
The morality of cursing depends on your viewpoint, your culture, and even your time and place in history. As mentioned

earlier, the Greeks and Romans cursed as part of everyday life and business. The Romans especially did not fool around. They demanded nothing short of destruction of their enemies in a curse. It is quite possible that their collective skill in cursing was one of the factors that enabled the Roman Empire to be created.

In today's society, cursing is considered immoral, perhaps even sinful. Yet, it does go on every day, in many ways we do not even recognize as such.

Breaking curses

There are many techniques for breaking curses, once the source has been identified. Here are some of the common ones:

Cleansing and binding cursed objects. An object believed to hold a curse or negative spirit attachment should be neutralized first. Simple but effective means of purification are to bathe the object in sunlight, or douse it in sea salt and then running water. Some people may prefer to use blessed salt and sprinklings of holy water. At the same time, spiritual help should be invoked through prayers and visualization.

For example, the object should be visualized as cleansed and pure, and the energy of the curse cleansed or dissipated

You may not know if a curse has been written. Writing a spell energizes it and helps to call forces into motion. (The same principle applies to affirmations for things you wish to manifest in your life.) However, you can use prayer and visualization to break up a possible written curse. Visualize the writing being burned by spiritual fire, or transformed in a positive way. Always see the negative energy transformed into positive energy.

Should curses be returned?

If you know who sent a curse, should you send it back to them? Opinions on this differ, but I believe that it is better to neutralize the curse and transform the energy, rather than send it back as a boomerang, and perpetuate the negativity.

Sources of help

Many people have the skills to deal with curses: exorcists, shamans, priests, ministers, psychics, mediums, Wiccans, Pagans, magicians, and so on. It is often useful to get a referral to such a person. Care must be taken, of course, for skills vary considerably. Beware of anyone who wants to charge you lots of money to lift a curse.

One of the best ways to deal with curse negativity is to build up your own spiritual protection to lessen your over-all vulnerability. Daily prayer and meditation will strengthen your aura and build stronger connections to your own sources of spiritual strength and help."

2

Haunted Objects

The doll had a burned face, but it was still collectible, and it was purchased by a husband and wife from a yard sale. It was placed in the couple's bedroom. Unbeknownst to them, the doll came with a nasty personality.

At night, the wife suffered mysterious bloody scratches on her legs. The attacks continued, and they sought the help of my friend, demonologist John Zaffis. The doll, they learned, had probably belonged to a little girl who died of burns from a fire. When they got rid of the doll, the bloody marks on the wife's legs disappeared.

The doll was possessed, though by what remains uncer-

to let them dry. I guess it bothered the spirit that I didn't put them away.

My son furnishes me with an entertainment center for my TV and two small end tables. I put one table at the closest wall of the living room. I put one of my cement statues on it. I put another statue on the other table. I am now alone again. In the night I hear the sound of something being put down on the table. A second later I hear it again. I go out of my room to expect to see something. Of course I see nothing. It sounds so much like my statues are being picked up and looked at, then put down again.

Another night I am lying in bed reading my Bible, which I did every night, and I pray for Tony and Bob (another past boyfriend). I start to cry because I can't control their problems. I love them both so much. I cry for a long time and feel so sad for them. They are such wonderful people. I close the Bible and put it down. I close my eyes. I feel a hand or hands straightening my pillow under my head. I freeze. I guess the spirit was trying to comfort me. But what a scary feeling of hands under my pillow moving under my head.

Friday night I go out to the local pub. I come home late. I start to doze off. Bang! Bang! Someone is pounding on the closet door right outside my bedroom. This made me jump out of bed. I said, "Whoever you are, this is my house. I need my sleep." It quit bothering me. I go back to sleep.

The next week I decide this mattress is what's keeping me from sleep. So I call the thrift store and they take it away. I burned sage that night and walked through every room praying that the spirit will leave me and go to a peaceful place.

Since that night I have had a quiet night every night.

Linda was fortunate that the problem was easily resolved. What was the troublesome spirit? Not likely a ghost – most ghosts are mere remnants of residual energy left behind when a person dies. Active presences usually are some type of spirit. Once the spirit starts to act up, it is advisable to take action, for the more it is allowed to be energized in an environment, the stronger it gets and the harder it is to banish.

Remedies

Remedies for possessed possessions to deactivate them include spiritual cleansings with salt, incense or sunlight, and blessings. Problems usually stop once the offending object is removed from the premises or destroyed, but in some cases home cleansings and blessings are needed as well.

If you are going to get rid of a possessed object, it is better to dispose of it rather than pass it on to someone else. Favored remedies are burial in the earth, disposal in deep water, and burning. If you take something to the local waste station, it will be burned, or compacted into a landfill, or even towed out to sea for dumping.

3

Mirrors: Doorways for Spirits

I have no mirrors in my bedroom. Not by chance – by choice. I work in the paranormal 24/7, and I am exposed to a wide range of activity, from benign to unpleasant. When I come home, I like psychic peace and quiet, especially when I sleep. Mirrors can be paranormal trouble spots – literal doorways for entities to enter your private physical space.

Mirrors, especially badly placed ones in bedrooms, sometimes are factors in some hauntings and attachments. I haven't had a mirror problem yet myself, but keeping them out of my bedroom is a preventative, considering the nature of my work. In fact, I have very few mirrors in my home at all.

Mirrors are not always a problem in the paranormal. They

are useful in scrying – clairvoyance in the present and future — and in psychic development. I teach mirror exercises in my intuition/psychic skills workshops. When it comes to problem hauntings, however, it is not surprising to find mirrors among the causes.

Ancient portals

Since ancient times, mirrors – or any shiny surfaces – have been regarded as portals to the unseen realms of spirits, the dead and the gods. They have facilitated clairvoyant visions of the past and future, and knowledge of the present. Spirits and the dead have been summoned to manifest in and through mirrors. Even today, people use mirrors in modern versions of the ancient psychomanteum, a place of oracular communication with the dead. Mirrors coated with black paint on the back are gazed at in dim light, positioned so that you cannot see your own reflection. In time, the eyes tire, and you enter a light altered state of consciousness. Spirits may appear in the mirror and be available for communication.

Psychomanteum work is undertaken in grief therapy, a topic explored by Raymond Moody in his book *Reunions*. Some years ago, I had the good fortune to spend a day with Raymond at his home in Alabama, where I underwent a psychomanteum session. Preparation for this was extensive, with Raymond and me processing my expectations and emotional considerations. The psychomanteum itself was in a small closet, with a large black-backed mirror set on the floor. A comfortable winged chair with the legs cut way down was positioned in a corner so that I could look into the mirror without seeing my own reflection. The walls were colored black. Dim light came from a small Tiffany lamp in another corner, the reflection of which also could not been seen when I looked into the mirror from the armchair. When the closet door was closed, the dim light was just enough to illuminate the mirror. My session, which I described at length in an article, was not as dramatic as some in *Reunions*, but was meaningful to me.

Black-coated mirrors also are used in psychic readings as scrying tools to see the future and things distant, and to communicate with the spirit realm. "Scrying" is derived from the English term *descry*, which means "to make out dimly" or "to succeed in discerning." Indeed, working with mirrors requires good discernment. As psychic tools, mirrors are neutral like any other interface. The results are determined by the user and circumstances.

Soul stealers

Mirrors may be neutral as tools, but they have a dark side in lore. In widespread belief, they are "soul stealers" with the power to suck souls out of bodies. In the Greek myth of Narcissus, he sees his own reflection in water, pines away and dies.

The devil and demonic entities can come through mirrors, according to lore. Actually, any spirit can use a mirror as a doorway into our world.

There also are numerous beliefs about mirrors and the dead. When a person dies, all the mirrors in a house should be turned over, for if a corpse sees itself in a mirror, the soul of the dead will have no rest or will become a vampire. Corpses who see themselves in mirrors also will bring bad luck upon the household. Such beliefs hark back to days when the corpses were laid out in homes, and people believed that souls lingered about the body until burial.

Another folk belief holds that if you see your own reflection in a room where someone has died, it is a death omen for yourself. Mirrors also should be covered in sick rooms in the folk belief that the soul is weakened and more vulnerable during illness.

By the way, the notion that vampires cannot see themselves in mirrors is fiction, not folklore, thanks to Bram Stoker and his novel *Dracula*. Stoker played on the widespread belief that evil entities have no soul, and thus there is nothing to reflect in a mirror. Count Dracula casts no reflection in mirrors, which is how Abraham Van Helsing exposes his true identity. This fiction has been discarded for the most part in modern vampire fiction, given the widespread presence of mirrors and reflective surfaces everywhere in society.

Mirrors in problem hauntings

If a home is plagued with unpleasant activity, presences, or atmosphere, check the location of mirrors, especially in bedrooms. Places where people sleep are considered to be the most vulnerable as entry points for spirits. Shadow People, who like to invade bedrooms, are often seen in mirrors and reflective surfaces.

Sometimes antique or secondhand mirrors with unknown histories can provide entry points. Consider the account of an Ontario, Canada woman who, as a teenager, kept a large antique mirror in her bedroom. The mirror had been passed down in her family. She became involved in Goth activities, and spent time in her room listening to dark, depressing music, doing dark writing, and keeping the room dimly lit with candles. One day she was in her room and suddenly the temperature plunged. She felt as though some unseen presence was looking out of the mirror at her. It frightened her, and she blew out the candles, turned on the electric lights, and moved the mirror to a spare room. Years later, she still owned the mirror, but was wary of it, and did not light candles in its presence.

A skeptic might argue that imagination is more at play in such cases than anything paranormal. The emotional tone set

were distracted by the real estate tension, or when we were pre-occupied with inspections. But after we were in and unpacking our boxes, I felt distinctly uncomfortable.

The house was a Cape Colonial style with dormer windows on the second floor, neat and attractive from the street, painted in iron gray with yellow trim. It was reasonably old by American standards, built in the 1920s. It had a beautiful field-stone fireplace, oak flooring and many original features, such as leaded glass French doors to the dining room.

The previous owners had seemed very happy with it. They had lived there only two years before a corporate transfer required them to move out of town.

The second night in the house, I had an odd experience as I was drifting off to sleep. I felt myself rise straight up off the bed in a prone position and hover near the ceiling. I was too frightened to open my eyes. And then just as suddenly, I was back on the bed.

Was it a quirky dream in the borderland state of consciousness? It would be impossible to rule that out. More likely, I had floated out-of-body.

We lived in the house for five years, and I never shook the feeling that I was constantly watched. It didn't seem that a ghost or ghosts lived in the house, but that the house itself had acquired a haunting personality. The *house* watched me.

I had bizarre dreams the entire time I lived there. I would hear strange noises, such as objects being dropped upstairs when I was the only person in the house. A common sound was the scattering of pins or small nails on the floor above me. Small things seemed oddly displaced at times – or was it just forgetfulness on my part?

I disliked being alone in the house, especially at night. And no matter what time of day or night, I disliked going down to the unfinished basement. The house seemed to literally breathe down there, and watch me with great intensity. Unfortunately, going to the basement was a necessity, as the laundry facilities were there.

My husband thought it was all my imagination, as he experienced nothing unusual in the house.

Then I learned a little about the house and the neighborhood. The house had had a frequent turnover of ownership. The neighborhood had been somewhat of a rum running center during the Prohibition days. Illegal whiskey had been stored in basements in various homes.

I often wondered if the house we now owned had had a

colorful history. And I often thought that if we hadn't been caught in a real estate boom, and had had more time to evaluate the house, we wouldn't have bought it, because I would have tuned in more to my discomfort.

Five years went by before it became financially feasible to move to a bigger house in Connecticut. We put the Westchester house up for sale. The market was much slower, but still viable. As soon as we listed the house, strange things began to happen on a more noticeable scale.

First it was little things going wrong. Something would break or not work right – especially of an electrical nature — which would affect the sales appeal of the house. We had a sudden onslaught of repairs to appliances, which would break down. We finally got a contract from prospective buyers – only to have it fall through when the buyers couldn't qualify for a loan. We lost valuable selling time.

One day we came home in the rain to find that our new roof inexplicably had sprung a major leak, ruining part of the ceiling, walls and carpeting upstairs. We had to take the house off the market for a considerable time while we made the repairs.

I got the feeling that the house did not want us to move. I discovered that in folklore, a house with frequent changes in ownership becomes unhappy and feels unloved. I wondered if our house wanted to hang onto us, even though I was not comfortable there. It certainly explained why I felt the house had its own personality.

Things came to a head when we landed another contract. This deal looked solid. We put a large, nonrefundable deposit down on a house in Connecticut. According to law in New York and Connecticut, buyers must put down 10 percent of the selling price, which can be forfeited to the sellers if they pull out or don't get a loan. The only legal "outs" are if the house does not pass engineering inspection or a radon gas test. Then the buyer can opt out and get the deposit back, or opt for remedies at the seller's expense.

Our house passed the engineer's inspection. I was elated – we were going to move! All we had left was the radon test – "a piece of cake," as our attorney assured us. Radon, a natural radioactive gas that leaches from the soil, is a problem in parts of the Eastern seaboard. Houses that test above a certain level must have a special, expensive venting system installed. People get freaky about radon and sometimes don't want anything to do with properties that test high in it, venting system or no. But in our neighborhood, houses had always tested well below the legal limit. And this house had been well below when we had purchased it.

When the radon test results came back, I was horrified. Not only were we above the limit, we were *five times* over it! Our attorney simply could not believe it. The testing company insisted the test had been administered properly. Now I feared the deal could fall through. I expected the buyers to bow out – they were a young couple who wanted to start a family. A radon-high house was not an attractive place.

Our attorney and real estate agent persuaded the sellers to allow the test to be re-administered. They argued that some had gone wrong with the test because the results were so out of line with the area.

But I knew the real problem – it was the house. It didn't want to let go.

The day of the test, I went around to every room in the house. I was angry. I shook my fist. I shouted, "We are going to move and you are going to let go of us. If you don't, I swear I will burn you to the ground!" And I meant it.

We passed the test well below the limit. The buyers were happy, and we closed the deal.

I never knew if the House With An Attitude made itself known to the new occupants. Hopefully, it was happy at last.

4

Drive-by Demons

Is it possible to call in a demon or any other entity, simply by thinking about it or writing about it? The answer is yes, technically you can. You do not need to do a ritual, work a Ouija board, or call out a name three times. Entities can tune in to thoughts and use them as homing beacons.

In practicality, beaming in entities is not all that easy, and stray thoughts here and there are not likely to bring anything to manifestation. Nor is reading about demons – and I believe it is important to be educated about them. I spend most of my time thinking about, researching, and writing about entities of all stripes and persuasions. If they all manifested at every thought and word, I would scarcely be able to get through the door of my home for the crowd there.

However, if you have the right intense mindset in the right environment and circumstances, you might find yourself host to unexpected visitors. Some of them are "drive-by" demons, a term I have coined to describe curious entities cruising by to see who is sending out an interest in them. I am using the term "demon" in the same way that the ancients did, to refer to a wide range of intermediary spirits who are capable of interacting – and interfering – with human beings. Not all demons are evil "servants of Satan." Some may be more mischievous than malevolent – but they can still cause distress.

I had an unusual drive-by visit from a powerful demon once, who honed in on me during a period of intense concentration of research and writing. The demon was Choronzon, the Demon of the Abyss, who figured in the sixteenth-century angel channeling work of John Dee and Edward Kelly, and who was later made famous by Aleister Crowley.

Coronzon (the original spelling in the angelic language given by Dee), also known as 333, is mentioned only once in Dee's diaries as the "mighty Devil" who orchestrates the expulsion of Adam and Eve from Paradise. Dee equated Choronzon with Satan himself. In the early twentieth century, Choronzon was an important figure in Crowley's magickal system – he added the "h" to the name. Choronzon is the Dweller of the Abyss and Demon of Dispersion, the last great obstacle to enlightenment.

The most famous story about Choronzon is the confrontation between the demon and Crowley and his ritual assistant, the poet Victor Neuberg, in the African desert in 1909. The men used Enochian calls, which are long invocations based on Dee's work, in a ritual for crossing the Abyss. They succeeded in evoking Choronzon. The ritual went out of control and the demon attacked Neuberg, physically fighting him with fangs and great fury. Neuberg was able to reassert control and subdue the demon, who eventually vanished back into his own realm.

Neuberg always insisted he physically fought the demon. Whether he did, or it was a visionary experience in an alternate reality, or (as some say) he struggled with a demon-possessed Crowley, will remain uncertain.

My own intersection with Choronzon came while I was working on *The Encyclopedia of Magic and Alchemy*. I was on the road, staying at someone else's home for several nights, packing my work with me as is my custom. While everyone else slept, I wrote well into the night. One night I devoted myself to the Crowley accounts of Choronzon, and went deep into concentration on the material.

I retired around 1:30 AM. and fell straight asleep. At about 3 AM, something bizarre happened. The perimeter safety lights around the house went on, waking up one of the occupants of the house (I'll call her Anne). The lights were set not to go off for dogs, raccoons and small animals, so something large had to be near the house. Anne got up with her dog and looked outside, but could see nothing. She walked into the living room, where I had been working, and felt a distinct, heavy, negative, unpleasant presence. The dog cowered and would not advance into the room.

Anne felt uneasy, but went back to bed, and slept fitfully the rest of the night. Amazingly, I slept through it all. Or, maybe it was not so amazing. After such intense concentration, I was more psychically open than usual, and something – probably the angels around me – protected me from being impacted.

In the morning, Anne told me what had happened. "It was weird and creepy," she said, and then gave me the eye. "You're not calling in any ETs, are you?"

I assured her I was not, and professed puzzlement over the episode. However, I knew right away what had happened. My intense concentration on Choronzon had gotten his attention, and he decided to drive by to see what was going on. Who was calling him?

I resolved to put aside the Crowley-Choronzon material until after I left, and especially to not work on anything related to Choronzon late at night. But the visits were not over.

The next night, I again retired around 1:30 and fell straight asleep. At around 3 AM the exact same scenario repeated itself, even though I had not been working on Choronzon or even demon subjects. It repeated a third time the following night. Anne said that the presence decreased both nights, as though something was gradually going away.

Again, I kept quiet, and surmised that my celestial protection had thrown a net around me.

The reinforcement of the number three was interesting. Choronzon is 333, and 3 AM is a common time for spirit manifestations. The visits repeated three times. In demonology, demons act in three's as a mocking of the Trinity.

Choronzon made no more attempts to visit – apparently his curiosity was satisfied that I was not a serious player in ritual magick attempting to summon him up. I had no more drive-bys during the rest of the work on the book. Nor did I have any drive-bys when I devoted two-plus years to researching and writing *The Encyclopedia of Demons & Demonology*. However, as a result of this experience, I was more careful about guarding myself, and about the circumstances under which I worked. I'm sure I was under surveillance by all kinds of spirits and demons, but I received no overt interference.

Choronzon was a stark demonstration to me that we truly do attract things according to the flow of our thoughts and intention. I have always felt that I have a good buffer around me – otherwise I could not pursue this work with great intensity – but even good buffers can be breached.

Any involvement in the paranormal, even occasional curiosity seeking, raises attention in the spirit realms. The more involved you are, the deeper you go, and the more you know, the more attention you attract. We may even get drive-bys we do not notice, for entities can hide their tracks. Choronzon chose not to come by stealth, but to make himself obvious. Perhaps he was irritated at the way I was yanking his chain.

How much is a person at risk for thinking about entities? We don't worry about angels and good entities, of course. We do worry about the dark side – but don't get paranoid. Reading, study, and inquiry in order to become informed and prepared are low-risk, and certainly are necessary for effective paranormal work. I think Choronzon showed up not only as a result of my concentration, but because of the long-standing nature of my work and the streams of consciousness I have developed for it, and because of the specific project.

Experimentation with ritual, spirit communication

devices, channeling and mediumship ups the risk ante. Have your protection in place and know what you're doing, and how to shut down the psychic centers and banish energy when you are done.

Deliberately summoning dark entities puts one at greater risk for an unpleasant encounter – and possibly attachment. Even experienced ritual magicians can have things go haywire on them. Evoking spirits is not a game. Demons and other dark entities are opportunists, and will zero in on people who might be vulnerable to their influence. Do not give them a reason.

6

The Djinn: Hide in Plain Sight

Some years ago, I became interested in an entity that is not very well known in the West, but which accounts for all manner of paranormal trouble in certain parts of the world, especially the Middle East: the Djinn. The word "Djinn" – also spelled Jinn — means "hidden ones," and it aptly describes these crafty master shape-shifters. After years of paranormal investigations and research, I came to the conclusion that, although the Djinn may have originated in Middle Eastern myth and lore, they are not limited by geography, any more than other entities are not limited in scope. They are everywhere, and they account for some of our more problematic haunting and possession cases.

Their universality applies to other entities, too. Various

cultures pay attention to certain entities and develop more lore about them than others, but the supernatural pays no attention to racial, cultural, or geographic boundaries. The fact that we know little about the Djinn in the West creates ideal circumstances for them to interact and interfere with us, all the while remaining disguised.

Every good paranormal investigator sooner or later has cases that resist explanation and resolution. The phenomena don't quite fit entities we are accustomed to encountering, and they don't respond to the banishing and exorcising methods we employ. Many of those difficult cases have Djinn behind them.

The Djinn can haunt houses, sites, and land. They can inhabit and attach to objects. They can attach to and even possess people. Some of them are tricksters who like to play pranks and make trouble; others have more of a mean streak and are bent on maximum torment. And some become infatuated or interested in humans and try to lend a helping hand.

The Djinn can act in demonic ways, but they are not demons. If they do not want to go, they will not. In a showdown between Djinn and humans, the Djinn are likely to have the upper hand.

Origins

According to pre-Islamic lore, the Djinn were born of smoke-less fire (which in modern terms could be plasma). They live very long lives but they are not immortal. According to some accounts, they live with other supernatural beings in the Qaf, a mythical range of emerald mountains that encircles the Earth. In modern terms, they live in a parallel dimension.

The Djinn are the "genies" in old folk tales known as the "Arabian Nights." In these stories, Djinn are trapped by magic in lamps and bottles, and when released they must grant three wishes before gaining their freedom. They always have a way of thwarting the wishes, hence the caution, "Be careful what you wish for." "Djinn" became "genie" when the tales were translated into French and English.

Our culture usually portrays genies in silly or humorous ways, which is probably why most Westerners do not take them seriously as real beings. Somewhere the Djinn are laughing back – our disbelief helps them remain hidden.

The Djinn also appear in legends of King Solomon, the second ruler of the Israelites. Solomon was granted power over spirits by God, and he enslaved the Djinn to build the Temple of Jerusalem. You won't find this story in the Bible, but it is told in detail in the ex-canonical text, the *Testament of Solomon.*

Solomon's magic became the basis for the Western magical tradition of commanding spirits.

Characteristics

The Djinn are invisible to most people except under certain conditions; however, animals, especially dogs and donkeys are able to see them. They can shape-shift into any form. They can masquerade as the ghosts of the dead and as other entities such as demons, fairies, elementals, and mysterious creatures. They can shape-shift into human guise. They may be exceptionally beautiful and exotic, or grotesque and ugly. They often like to take shapes that will upset and shock humans, such as mysterious creatures. They appear and disappear as smoke and mist. They have long been regarded as malicious and dangerous, capable of bringing bad luck, illness, disaster and death. Even when granting favors, they have a trickster nature and can twist events for the worse.

In Middle Eastern lore, the Djinn like to roam the deserts and wilderness and inhabit caves. There are many other places on the Earth to their liking: remote, mountainous areas, places full of old mine tunnels, deserts, valleys, swamps, and areas where the natural Earth energy is agreeable to them. These are spots where the magnetic energy is likely to be much lower than surrounding areas: a negative magnetic anomaly.

Djinn in Muslim lore

Islamic theology absorbed the Djinn, and an entire chapter in the Qur'an, *al-Jinn (The Jinn)*, concerns them. According to Islam, humans were created from clay and water, and angels from a special and pure spiritual light. Djinn were created from smokeless fire.

The Djinn were created before man. By some accounts, they were created two thousand years before Adam and Eve, and were equal to angels in stature; they had access to heaven. When Allah created Adam, he told the angels to bow to his new creation. The angels complied, but Iblis, the leader of the Djinn, refused on the grounds that Adam was inferior. This angered Allah, and he cursed the Djinn and cast them out. Iblis appealed to Allah for a chance to prove he was right, that humans were flawed. The Djinn were granted the opportunity to redeem themselves by Judgment Day.

Some Djinn accepted their fate and new world, while others were angry, and wanted revenge against humans.

Iblis (also called Shaytan) became a figure comparable to the Devil. His evil-minded followers are called devils, and they behave in ways similar to Western demons, which probably accounts for some of the Western confusion about them. The Djinn are not demons, and they are not fallen angels. However,

it may be a Djinn. The Djinn are very territorial, and the ones that latch on to real estate in our dimension resent the presence of people. They preceded humans and feel they have land rights here. They view us as the invaders and squatters on their territory. They are not interested in sharing, or peaceful co-existence; they just want people to go away, and will try to make them miserable until they do. If the Djinn communicate in such circumstances, their message is likely to be one of eminent domain: "I was here first, this is my territory, and I want you to leave."

Demons can do all of the above as well, but their purpose is often a battle for the soul. Djinn may not have an interest in your fate in the afterlife. They may, however, be interested in using your life force or soul energy for their own purposes, or in fooling you into thinking you are dealing with a demon.

And finally, if a variety of expulsion methods have been tried and have failed, the culprit is probably a Djinn. They can be quite tenacious. Weaker ones may throw in the towel, but those that are strong and determined can wear down most human beings.

Remedies against Djinn

There are many protections against Djinn and exorcism rituals, and some may work to push them out. Every situation has its own dynamics of the individual interests and power of the entity involved, the reasons for interfering with people, the energy of place, and the wild card of the humans involved.

In the Middle East, the blue eye amulet is one of the most common charms against unwanted spirits. Various prayers are said to be effective as well. There are bargaining tactics, but bargaining with entities is quite dangerous and can lead to more trouble. It may be necessary to summon someone who has had experience dealing with the Djinn and knows how to ritually expel them.

The Djinn seem to be sensitive to electrical and electro-magnetic fields. When they are in Shadow People form, they are sometimes repelled by lights, and by the running of devices such as televisions and computers.

The Djinn are not new to our paranormal situations; they have merely been below our radar for a long time. It will take us some time to learn how to deal with them.

7

Shadow People:
Terror in the Bedroom

Tall, sinister, black figures that stand by the bed at night and stare intensely at us. Black silhouettes that peek around doorways and wall corners. Flitting dark forms in haunted locations. They are all called Shadow People. Our gut reaction to them: Fear. Panic. Terror.

Are they dark ghosts of human beings, or some other entities? Whoever they are, why do they seem so intensely interested in us? And why do they terrify us so badly? Demons often pale by comparison when it comes to the fear invoked by a Shadow Person.

My curiosity about Shadow People led me to initiate a

project, soliciting personal experiences and researching the phenomenon against folklore, paranormal literature, mythology, other documented entity contact experiences, and so on. I have collected hundreds of cases of Shadow People that reveal complex patterns of appearances and behavior. Shadow People are one of the most common, most mysterious and most scary of all paranormal experiences. And we have very few answers.

In the course of my research and paranormal investigations, I have had numerous encounters with Shadow People. Inquire about them, and they show up. They are huge and intimidating, and on occasion I have made an exit rather than stay in the presence of one.

Characteristics

There are different types of Shadow People. The core, dominant experience is the nighttime bedroom visitor: a tall silhouette of a man, often dressed in a coat or cape, and a brimmed hat. The figure is blacker than black and three-dimensional, obstructing light and blocking the view of objects. There are no facial features or eyes (although sometimes red eyes are reported), but the experiencer *knows* he is being observed with great intensity. The Shadow Person does not communicate, but often radiates an intense malevolent, trickster, or evil energy.

In the typical experience, a person wakes up from sleep

and sees a Shadow Person in the bedroom. It stands right at the bedside, in a corner, or in the doorway. It may emerge from a closet or slide out from under the bed. Some of them come through the walls.

The experiencer is usually terrified and screams. A reaction often makes the Shadow Person disappear, either by vanishing into thin air, zipping down a hallway, or melting through a wall or ceiling (or back under the bed!). They move with lightning speed, gliding, sliding and teleporting themselves. People may feel paralyzed to do anything but shut their eyes, hoping that the figure will be gone when they open them. Sometimes it is – and sometimes it isn't.

Some people feel extremely threatened by the Shadow Person. It sits on the bed, or presses on them with suffocating or choking intensity. The experience usually ends before actual physical harm occurs, but the lingering terror takes a severe psychological toll.

Some Shadow People are less formed, and are more like pillars or vertical blobs of black. The indistinct forms may be the result of the fleeting way they are often seen: out of the corner or the eye, or briefly as they zip from one spot to another. Even if they do not exhibit a marked human-like shape, victims still feel a watching, intelligent and hostile presence.

Other kinds of Shadow People start as shadows on the wall. It takes a moment for a person to realize that the shadow is unnatural and should not be there – and then the shadow starts to move. It materializes from the wall into physical space and takes on a three-dimensional form.

Shadow People also have been reported in wooded areas. In America, accounts of them go back to old Indian lore. They always seem to be watching... for *something*. In Northern California, the Watchers are tall, black silhouettes of men wearing capes and large floppy brimmed hats. They stand on lonely cliffs and watch into the distance.

Another category of Shadow People are dark figures seen in some haunted places. Waverly Hills Sanatorium in Louisville, Kentucky, and Eastern State Penitentiary in Philadelphia are famous for them. Some paranormal investigators believe these figures are dark ghosts or thought-forms that are part of the haunting phenomena present on site. That is possible, but I think it is more likely that the chaotic psychic energy in such places provides an energy source to Shadow People.

Silent but intelligent

Shadow People rarely communicate, which makes them even more unnerving to confront. Witnesses are at a loss to under-stand who they are and what they want. Sometimes they communicate an intention, telepathically, that is hostile, and makes the victim feel that harm is imminent.

Despite their silence, witnesses are certain they are extremely intelligent, more so than human beings, and that they have a purpose and agenda for tracking us. "Evil incarnate," one experiencer told me.

Looking for patterns

Shadow People experiences are not gender biased — men and women experience them fairly equally. Nor is there a noticable age bias. Experiences range from early childhood to late in life. Some people have one or two experiences they never forget, and others are "serial experiencers," having irregular, unpredictable experiences and attacks that keep them on a psychological edge. There are solo witnesses, multiple witnesses, and family omen-type Shadow People that follow generations.

Sometimes Shadow People are attached to a place. In such cases, Shadow People experiences start when people move to a certain location, and stop when they leave. Sometimes Shadow People are attached to individuals or even families, following them wherever they go. Sometimes Shadow People are bad omens, almost like banshees. The appearance of the Shadow Person forecasts a run of bad luck. Other Shadow People experiences seemed linked to states of emotional turmoil.

Possible explanations

Like many paranormal phenomena, Shadow People do not fall into a single neat category. They share characteristics of different types of phenomena or entities. Here are some of the explanations I have examined. I am convinced that Shadow People are none of these, although they embody some of the characteristics of each type of entity:

Ghosts: Many haunted places have dark ghosts. Their dark appearances may be due to their ability to manifest – they may be low on our threshold of awareness – or they may embody a psychic essence of turmoil or violence. Haunting shadow figures are different from Shadow People. Dark figures often repeat their actions or lurk in small areas.

Thought-forms: Thought-forms are coalesced emotions, such as residual energy that collects in a place over time and becomes imprinted into the psychic space, or are projections from the living. Some of my respondents have volunteered that they think their own dark emotional states have caused or influenced their experiences. I do not think the Shadow People are thought-forms, but I do think that emotional turmoil provides an energy that attracts them. Perhaps they vampirize fear and turmoil, converting it into an energy that is useful to them.

Astral entities or demons: The malevolence radiated by most Shadow People have led many experiencers to interpret them as demonic or low-level astral beings. Such entities can take on a shape-shifted form in order to create havoc. However, Shadow People are well-organized as a distinct phenomenon. They do not always react to religious invocations, prayers and objects.

Nightmare hags: The dark forms, bedside appearances, paralysis and suffocating feelings are similar to attacks by the nightmare hag, which presses on people in bed in a suffocating manner, and sometimes is visible as a monstrous black form. As mentioned, some Shadow People are not well-shaped as humans but are more blobs or pillars of black, inky swirls. Nightmare hags are not observers, however, and lack the sophisticated sets of behaviors and auras of intelligence possessed by Shadow People.

Vampires: In folklore, the vampire is a restless ghost or an entity that sucks off the life force, usually while victims sleep. There is a small overlap here with Shadow People, as experiencers often feel drained – perhaps by the sheer fright of the experience.

Ultraterrestrials: Shadow People may be unknown beings from other dimensions that layer ours, an explanation proposed for mysterious creatures such as Mothman and Bigfoot. They do seem to slide at will between our world and another.

An extraterrestrial connection?

An unexpected turn in my data collection shows a strong connection between Shadow People and extraterrestrials. Shadow People bear a strong resemblance to Men in Black, who look like odd men dressed all in black suits and black hats. MIB visit ET/UFO experiencers and warn them not to talk to others. Some ufologists think that MIB are related to government monitoring, but their weird appearance and robot-like ways – as well as their ability to appear and disappear without explanation – point in a paranormal direction.

ETs who are abductors – the little grays with big black eyes – are bedroom visitors, coming while people sleep. They sometimes come through walls or materialize in rooms, and they cause paralyzing fright and terror.

I have found that people who are frequent experiencers of Shadow People have also had significant or frequent ET experiences, ranging from sightings to bedroom invasions to abductions. The exact nature of the relationship between the two entities is unknown. Possibilities are:

Shadow People are monitors for ETs. They may be artificial intelligence or drones programmed to monitor our thoughts and consciousness, information that may be useful to the ETS. It may be easiest for them to do this while we are asleep, which is why they appear as nighttime visitors. They may be programmed to disappear when they are observed.

Shadow People are separate entities working in cooperation with ETs. Alliances among human beings are common, and the same may apply to other entities. Some ufologists and others believe we are already well into contact stages with other entities. Their motives can include hybridization, mining the natural resources of the Earth, and colonization. Perhaps Shadow People have a stake in the process.

Shadow People are separate entities monitoring ET activity on Earth. In this scenario, Shadow People have their own goals and objectives concerning Earth and humans, and are keeping tabs on the ET agendas. It is interesting to note that ETs and Shadow People seldom show up at the same time. Perhaps Shadow People are capable of identifying ET targets and tagging them for their own monitoring.

The Djinn connection

The form of Shadow People makes a good fit with the Djinn, who like to stay hidden behind shape-shifted or mysterious presences. In addition, as noted earlier in this book, some of the Djinn are hostile to humans and have their own agendas to pursue. They like to take energy from people, which they may be able to accomplish by provoking fear and terror. They may wish to know more about us, biologically, emotionally and mentally, in pursuit of their purposes in our world. Remember, according to lore, they once had the planet as theirs, and lost it to us. From that perspective, the ET associations with experiencers makes sense. Perhaps the Djinn and ETs are in competition with each other concerning humans.

Djinn like disguises and shapes that upset humans. The coat or cloak may be deliberate, or may conceal their true shape. Experiencers are often puzzled about the hats of Shadow People. Why would an entity intent on terrorizing people wear odd and out of fashion hats? There is a comical element to it. The Djinn are supreme tricksters, but there may be another reason for hats: they may cover up something about the heads of the entities that cannot otherwise be shape-shifted or hidden. Some Shadow People have misshapen heads, regardless of whether or not they seem to wear hats. Experiencers have volunteered to me that they have a strong feeling that the true form of Shadow People is something so hideous that humans would not be able to stand it.

The stealthy behavior of Shadow People suits the Djinn as well. When the Djinn interfere with humans, they lurk and build fear, or strike without warning. Shadow People exhibit both kinds of behavior.

Shadow People seem to have the best fit with Djinn. Still,

that does not mean that all Shadow People are Djinn. It may only mean that Shadow People are a favorite form borrowed by the Djinn to throw us off their track.

Remedies

There are no consistent, universally reliable and guaranteed measures against Shadow People visits and attacks. Some measures work for some people and not for others. Repeat experiencers have to experiment until they find the best solution. In some cases, people cannot get rid of the entities, but can minimize their intrusions.

Turning on lights works for many people. As soon as a light goes on, a Shadow Person is likely to exit or disappear. They may have difficulty staying in the presence of electrical and electromagnetic fields generated by lights and other devices. Some serial experiencers find that visits are minimized by regularly sleeping with a light on, and also by keeping a television, radio, stereo or computer on in the bedroom.

Religious measures work for some people. Reciting prayers, such as the Lord's Prayer, and invoking the help of God, spiritual figures such as Jesus, the Virgin Mary, saints and so on, send some Shadow People away. Organized religion likes to insist that religion will always work against unwanted presences, but in truth that is not always the case.

What are skinwalkers?

In Native American lore, skinwalkers are evil sorcerers who shape-shift into animal and other forms and travel about very rapidly, especially at night. They cause illnesses, incite people to violence, rob graves and kill people. The land occupied by the Skinwalker Ranch, as the place is known, is in the Uinta Basin, an area famous for supernatural lore and activity. According to local lore, the ranch violates skinwalker pathways, making it an unlucky place. Locals either avoid speaking of skinwalkers or talk about them in hushed tones so as not to attract their unwanted attention.

The Navajo called skinwalkers the *yenaldlooshi*. Both men and women can be skinwalkers. They meet secretly at night in caves to plan their evil activities, according to lore. Bullets supposedly go right through them when they are in shape-shifted form, unless one aims for the neck.

A broader definition of skinwalkers is found in occult lore, holding that they can be the shape-shifted forms of nonhuman entities, such as the Djinn and perhaps demonic entities. These beings, like their human sorcerer counterparts, also have malevolence in mind.

Drama at the ranch

The paranormal perils at Skinwalker Ranch probably go back a very long time, but did not become documented prior to the 1990s. In 1994, a rancher pseudonymously named Tom Gorman and his family found the ranch in the Uinta Basin and thought it was their dream come true. Tired of small town life in New Mexico, they yearned for a more comfortable and private place to raise their expensive cattle. But instead of a happy dream, their experience was, from the beginning, a nightmare.

Curiously, the ranch home had an excessive number of bolts and locks, as though the previous owners had been desperate to keep something out. Country and ranch folk often don't lock their doors, but the previous residents seemed to want a barricade. After the Gormans moved in, they discovered what was so unwanted and feared.

Mysterious invisible shapes moved about the landscape, like rushes of wind. Sometimes forms were barely visible. Flying lights appeared. An excessively large wolf menaced the cattle and was not felled — or even wounded — by point-blank rifle fire. Poltergeists kept moving things about the ranch house. And most strangely of all, they witnessed an orange mass in the western sky sometimes at night, which tore open to show blue sky within, as though they were peering into a porthole to another world.

Fast-moving flying objects, including a black one, were seen emerging from this hole in the sky. Gorman became convinced that his ranch was the site of some kind of dimensional doorway for these flying objects.

The Gormans learned that the Ute Indians would not venture onto the land because they considered it cursed. According to native lore, skinwalkers used this land for their travelways to and from Dark Canyon, their dwelling place not far away. But the phenomena experienced by the Gormans seemed to extend far beyond human sorcery, involving unknown creatures from other dimensional realities.

As the family settled into life on the ranch, the phenomena escalated. Something intelligent was behind everything, giving it direction, and responding to the Gormans' fear and anger. Efforts to banish whatever was plaguing them only brought more trouble upon them. Cattle were mutilated and also disappeared. In an emotionally disturbing episode, Tom Gorman's favorite dogs ran off chasing mysterious blue orbs. Gorman later found them horribly incinerated; all that remained of them were smears of grease.

Word of these goings-on spread, and attracted the attention of the National Institute for Discovery Science (NIDS), established by real estate and aerospace entrepreneur Bob Bigelow. Bigelow founded NIDS with the purpose of scientifically investigating UFOs and other high strangeness. (NIDS is now dismantled.) In 1996, NIDS bought the ranch and organized a team of scientists to set up a scientific investigation. The Gormans left.

The scientists had plenty of bizarre eye-witness experiences themselves, but were unable capture conclusive hard data, even after years of work – or so they said. It was as though whatever was behind the phenomena could by-pass all their surveillance gear. Nonetheless, their efforts were not in vain, but raise serious questions about our views on reality.

A report on the Skinwalker Ranch was published in a book, *Hunt for the Skinwalker: Hunt for the Skinwalker: Science Confronts the Unexplained at a Remote Ranch in Utah*, written by Colm A. Kelleher, one of the scientist investigators, and George Knapp, an award-winning television broadcaster in Las Vegas. Some ufologists contend that the scientists did get hard evidence, which was withheld. And, they say, not all of the phenomena were reported. What was left out was stranger still.

Speculation aside, what is documented is quite chilling. On one occasion at night, one of the NIDS investigators witnessed a yellow light manifest on the property, which turned into a tunnel. A large black humanoid creature about six feet tall with no facial features crawled out of the tunnel and walked away on the ranch. The tunnel shrank and disappeared, leaving behind a pungent smell of sulphur. Many people automatically associate sulphur with the demonic, but more likely is it is an effect of some interdimensional openings.

The NIDS investigators witnessed other phenomena, but reportedly were never able to capture any of it on camera, due to mysterious malfunctions and destruction of equipment. It seemed as though whatever was causing the phenomena played a cat and mouse game with them.

Some of the investigators became ill after spending time on the property. Symptoms included severe headaches and weakness.

After several years, NIDS officially ended its investigation, saying it had "very little physical evidence of anomalous phenomena, at least no physical evidence that could be considered proof of anything. This was in spite of hundreds of days of human monitoring and several years of camera surveillance."

Even though the investigation was officially ended, phenomena there and in the area continue. Local researchers say the ranch is used by ETs, and there are tunnels below the surface. They see continuing anomalous aerial lights and activity in the vicinity of the ranch.

The ranch is off limits to visitors. It is completely fenced, with surveillance cameras and microphones set up at the main gate.

Is the Skinwalker Ranch a portal or doorway to other dimensions? It would seem so, and probably is but one of many that dot the planet. The chilling aspect of these portals is that other beings seem to be able to use them at will to intrude upon us and our reality.

9

Doppelgangers:
The Shock of Seeing Double

One of the most shocking experiences a person can have is meeting your own exact self. Not someone who bears a strong resemblance to you, but an exact duplicate. This eerie double goes by many names, including doppelganger (a German term meaning "double-goer"), fetch and wraith. Whatever the label, the appearance of a doppelganger often bodes ill.

Doppelgangers have been recorded for centuries, and a wealth of folklore exists about them. According to lore, seeing your own double means misfortune is about to descend upon you and your family. In the most extreme, seeing yourself means you will die soon. Shortly before he drowned in a storm off the coast of Italy on July 8, 1822, the English poet Percy

Bysshe Shelley had a disturbing vision of seeing his own double, which asked him, "How long do you mean to be content?" His double was seen by others as well.

Doppelgangers can appear as solid, flesh-and-blood figures that walk and talk like the real person. Some of them are semi-transparent, or move in odd ways without talking.

No one knows why doubles appear, especially prior to deaths and personal disasters. If doppelgangers are warnings, why do they not appear to everyone? Perhaps the shock would be too great for most people.

Not all doppelgangers are bad omens, however. Many cases on record are benign and are not associated with disasters and death — but many also are without obvious explanation or reason. Some people spontaneously and unwittingly have a bilocation, a projection of a part of themselves that seems real to others.

Bilocation is a supernormal ability in mystical traditions, and some adepts, including saints, do it at will. St. Padre Pio, for example, was well known for bilocations of his double. It seems the saint would be called out, especially while he was sleeping, to aid others in distress.

Some doppelgangers are called "arrival cases" by psychical

researchers, because the double appears in advance of the arrival of a person at a location. Many accounts of arrival cases were collected by the Society for Psychical Research in London around the turn of the twentieth century. One famous case involved the author Mark Twain, who went to a reception and dinner where he met a woman he knew. However, the real woman was not there — she was on board a train traveling to the event at the time that Twain encountered her.

Louis Rodgers was an English medium living in Australia in the early twentieth century who had the ability to project his realistic double at will to distant locations. He could send his doppelganger to hotels to check in before he got there. Rodgers participated in experiments with psychical researchers to document his ability.

Are doppelgangers evil? There is nothing in the literature of actual cases to indicate so, but in film and fiction they make good villains, running amok and wreaking havoc. Perhaps the doppelganger embodies our fears that we have a dark side that lies beyond our control and waits for an opportunity to take on a life of its own.

10

Beware the Ghost
Who Calls Your Name

Ever hear a disembodied voice call your name out loud? If so, take care — it may be a bad spirit luring you to doom.

At least, that is the explanation given in a long tradition of folklore. "Calling ghosts" speak out the name of a person to attract his attention. Sometimes people who live in or investigate haunted places hear their names called out,, but no one is visible.

In folklore, calling ghosts lure people to their deaths. They are related to evil-minded spirits in mythology, as such the sirens of Greek lore: water nymphs whose beautiful singing lured sailors to their deaths. The sirens lived on an island between Circe's isle and Scylla. They sat on a flower bed surrounded by the rotting corpses of the men they killed.

In Homer's *Odyssey*, the hero Odysseus has to sail past the sirens. He orders his men plug their ears with wax so they will not be lured onto rocks that would destroy the ship. But Odysseus wants to hear the song himself, so he has himself tied to his ship's mast as it sails past the sirens. He risks madness to do so.

In Hawaiian lore, calling ghosts are disembodied female voices who call your name behind you. When you turn around, you make yourself vulnerable to illness or death.

Calling ghosts are the basis of a superstition that you should never respond to a stranger who calls out your name — he might be a bad-omen calling ghost in disguise.

11

Dream Invasion

You wake up in the middle of the night and know that there is something ugly, perhaps even unholy, in the room. You can't see it, but you know it's there. It comes closer, making shuffling and snorting sounds, and then suddenly you see red eyes as a "thing" comes down on the bed — or even on top of you.

You are paralyzed in terror, cannot move, cannot even scream. Then suddenly it is gone... or else things go black... and you wake up in the morning and wonder what happened. Was it a nightmare — or a real experience?

Nighttime entity attacks like this have been going on in the human race since ancient times.

and malevolent. They are capable of entering dreams to influence thoughts or cause upsetting nightmares.

Hags. In earlier times, people believed that witches, or hags, caused nightmares by stealing into a bedroom and sitting on a person's chest. To be "hag-ridden" meant having nightmares all night long. Hag attacks involve frightening, unknown presences that can be smelled, heard, felt and sometime seen. The victim feels paralyzed and may feel choked or suffocated. The victim may feel awake, or may be uncertain if the experience is a waking one or a dreaming one. In addition, there may be nightmares of violence.

Hag attacks, also called the Old Hag syndrome, have been studied, but there is no single explanation that can account for them. They have been blamed on nightmares, diet, medications, mood disorders, sleep paralysis, narcolepsy, sexual repression, emotional trauma and other natural causes. When you come down to it, however, supernatural causes can't be ruled out.

Folklorist David J. Hufford, author of *The Terror That Comes in the Night* (1982),estimates that about fifteen percent of the general population worldwide suffers at least one hag attack during life. Some individuals suffer attacks several times a year. Rarely, individuals suffer frequent attacks over a limited period of time. Even rarer are those who suffer frequent and chronic attacks. Knowledge or belief in the Old Hag does not influence whether or not people have the experience. Hag attacks can happen during daytime naps as well as at night.

A hag attack is terrifying, but ends before anything bad happens. In some cases, the victim feels sexually assaulted. The victim may feel as though he is having a lucid dream, or may be uncertain whether he is awake or dreaming, or may feel completely awake. The victim often awakens in the morning feeling drained and exhausted.

According to Hufford, hag attacks have played a significant role in the development of supernatural lore, including the incubus and succubus, both sexual predator demons, and the vampire, a sexual predator and drainer of the life force.

People. Certain people have the ability and power to invade another person's dreams by projecting an intention, casting a spell or throwing a curse. "Dream sending" has been practiced since ancient times. The objective is to wear down a person's well-being and cause physical and psychological torment and destruction.

Telling the difference in dreams

How do you distinguish an invaded dream from an ordinary dream? Everyone has occasional nightmares that are part of normal dreaming, including unpleasant landscapes and monstrous creatures. If you pay attention to your dreams, you can recognize certain signs and elements that indicate invasion. For example, the invaded dream may have unusual, ugly chaos and violence in it, like bloody killing and mutilation. The "tone" of it might be intensely oppressive. There may be distorted, misshapen people, and monsters or monstrous forms. All of those elements can be in an ordinary dream, but the difference is often the way the elements all fit together, combined with a certain "feel" that may be physical, too, that tips the difference.

Invaded dreams may have the same theme or elements that repeat night after night. And, the dream invasion may follow on the heels of paranormal activity, such as an investigation, rituals gone awry, or attempts at spirit communication that leave a person too psychically open.

Invaded dreams also differ from spirit visitation dreams. We can have realistic dream encounters with the recently dead, who appear in dreams to give reassurance to us that they are all right in the afterlife. These visitation dreams are positive and healing. Other benevolent visitation dreams involve angels, spiritual masters and spirit guides. Their purpose, too, is to provide help and healing.

Invaded dreams are not helpful, but quite distressful. How

likely are they to happen? It depends on a person's vulnerability and the circumstances involved. I don't think there is cause to be overly worried about the possibility. When dealing with the paranormal, it is always a good idea to be aware of the various things that can happen, however.

Banishing dream invasion

In some cases, dream invasion goes away on its own after a night or two. Residual ghosts attached to haunted places usually stay put, and affect only those who sleep in certain rooms. When you leave the place, the problem stops.

A spirit capable of attachment may run out of juice outside of its original haunting environment, and its effect will fade away. In other cases, the spirit is energized by its attachment, and can cause a variety of miseries, from haunting phenomena to poltergeist disturbances to unpleasant dreams – and more.

Demonic and Djinn cases require expert help. Many hag attack dreams are of unknown origins – some people experience them repeatedly throughout their lives, and learn various ways of coping.

In cases of suspected psychic attack, a person can take measures to repel the invasion. Mental techniques of visualizing yourself surrounded by impenetrable armor, reflective mirrors and cocoons of light can help to end dream invasion. Also helpful are spiritual cleansings of prayer or meditation, plus a forceful order to the offending spirit to depart. An energy healing session can clear the aura and restore balance. A cleansing of place may be necessary if the problem lingers. In demonic cases, let the experts deal with the situation.

Get dream savvy

If you desire to have a deep involvement in the paranormal, it is a good idea to learn about your dreams, for they are an important interface to nonphysical realms. According to scientific research, dreams are the most likely medium for psi. In a study in the 1963 of ten thousand cases of psi, parapsychologist Louisa Rhine found that fifty-seven percent of them occurred in dreams. Rhine suggested that dreams may be the most efficient carriers of psi, because in sleep the barriers to the conscious mind appear to be thinnest.

Pay attention to your dreams on a regular basis and learn dreamwork techniques so that you can distinguish an unusual dream from an ordinary dream.

If you think you are having invaded dreams that persist, get expert help. First rule out natural causes, such as underlying psychological factors. Consult someone such as a clinical psychologist who is knowledgeable about dreams *and* the paranormal (some psychologists will dismiss paranormal possibilities). If you think there paranormal factors are involved, find someone in your area who can help. Most metaphysical and occult bookstores know practitioners in their areas, and may be able to make referrals.

Ghost, demon – or something else?

Is a sexually predatory spirit really a ghost? Various explanations have been put forward. All of them have possibility, but there is virtually no way to prove one explanation over the other. In the end, we are left with anecdotal testimony – the impressions and convictions of the experiencer.

Demons have been blamed for sexual visits for centuries. In fact, some people believe that ghosts do not have sex, and demons masquerading as the dead are the real culprits. Sexual encounters with demonic and nonhuman spirits are well documented in anecdotal lore. Most famous are the incubus and succubus, male and female demons respectively, that force sexual encounters upon their victims. These demonic entities masquerade as beautiful and alluring people, even ghosts, in order to fool their victims and accomplish their goals.

Demonic sexual assaults are unpleasant, even horrifying. The 1983 film *The Entity*, starring Barbara Hershey, is a terrifying portrayal of demonic assault and rape, based on a true account. The identity of the entity and the reasons for its sudden onset of attacks are never known.

Other entities besides ghosts and demons have histories of sexual activity with humans. Fairies are famous for it, often becoming infatuated with people. The Djinn, a supernatural race of shape-shifting beings, also like to engage in sex with people. Extraterrestrial contactees report a variety of sexual encounters, including forced sex for the apparent purpose of creating hybrids, as well as pleasant sexual encounters more like ghostly sex. People have even reported sex with humanoid-reptilian beings, who either live below the surface of the earth or come from another off-world realm.

One of the most famous supernatural sexual partners is the vampire. I'm referring to real vampires, not Lestat, or even Count Dracula. The real vampire, documented in anecdotal literature, is an entity that vampirizes the living of its life force. The vampire might be the monstrous spirit of the human dead who does not make a successful crossing to the afterlife, and is doomed to wander the earth looking for satisfaction, at least for a time. Vampires can also be nonhuman entities. According to popular fiction and film, the vampire always takes blood, but in real-life cases from the past, the vampire was just as likely to prefer sex to blood. In fact, sometimes that was how the vampire killed its victim – exhaustion from too much sex!

The hag

Ghost sex also gets mixed with another entity assault called the hag attack, discussed in more detail in a separate chapter. This, too, has been documented since ancient times. The dominant characteristics are awakening to find a horrible, unknown presence in the room that comes close or gets on the bed, and being paralyzed, unable to even scream. Hag attacks get their name from the belief in earlier centuries that witches, or hags, sat on people at night, caused nightmares, and left them drained and exhausted by morning. Victims may see dark shapes, hear snorting and shuffling, and smell foul odors.

A woman once described to me how she was hag-attacked periodically throughout her life. Sexual assault was involved. She called the entity "It," and could not make it go away for years. After her husband died, she was terrified that "It" would have complete reign over her. On its next visit, she screamed at It to go away and leave her alone – something she had done in the past, but apparently this time she did it with enough force. It went away without molesting her, and never returned.

Can ghost sex be explained naturally?

Psychiatric problems, sexual repression, mood swings and drugs have been advanced as natural explanations for ghost sex. The argument is made that the sexual encounter seems real, but is imaginary and a projection – perhaps even a residue of dreaming. Many experiencers are uncertain if they've had a vivid dream that seemed real, or a real encounter.

However, there is plenty in anecdotal lore to bolster the argument that human ghosts engage in real, not imaginary, sex.

When ghost sex is welcome

The literature on "after-death communications" (ADC), or visitations by people who are dead, includes accounts of sex. Most cases of ADC involve visitations in dreams, in which the dead person assures a friend or loved one that he or she is all right. In some cases, the visitations get physical – a dead husband, wife or lover returns at night to the bed, and it is not a dream.

Such experiences are explained away by therapists as projections due to loneliness and grief. Privately, however, some experiencers disagree, and say they welcome the visits.

An odd case of sex from beyond the grave involves reincarnation as well, told in *The Search for Omm Sety* (1987) by Jonathan Cott. Dorothy Eady, an Englishwoman, believed she had been a lover of the Egyptian pharaoh, Omm Sety I, who lived from 1306-1290 BCE. Her past-life memories began at an early age. Eady moved to Egypt, and recorded in her diaries that Sety, in ghostly or astral form, resumed his love affair with her, eventually coming to her nightly.

In a bizarre twist, she told him he could keep visiting, but they would have to stop having sex. She had to atone for breaking virginal vows as a young priestess in that long-ago life. Eady died in 1981. Perhaps she has rejoined her soul mate in Amenti, the halls of the Underworld.

13

The Evil Eye: A Killing Look

The popular expression "if looks could kill" is not just an idle turn of phrase. Since ancient times, certain people have possessed a lethal power with their eyes. With a glance, they bring misfortune, disaster, illness – and even death.

The "look" is called the evil eye, and it is no joke. Folklore around the world is full of protections and remedies to keep a baleful look from bringing doom and death.

The oldest recorded reference to the evil eye dates to about 3000 BCE in the cuneiform texts of the Sumerians, Babylonians and Assyrians. The ancient Egyptians believed in it, and used eye shadow and lipstick to prevent the evil eye from entering their eyes or mouths. The Bible makes references to the evil eye in both Old and New Testaments. It is among ancient Hindu folk beliefs. Evil eye superstitions are still strong in parts of the world, especially in Mediterranean countries such as Italy, and in Mexico and Central America.

Who possesses the evil eye? Traditionally, magically empowered people such as witches, sorcerers and shamans have the power and use it to curse and punish. Deliberate evil eye is also called "overlooking," and is a form of witchcraft that can bring about misfortune, catastrophe, illness, poverty, injury, loss of love, and even death. During the witchcraft hysteria that gripped Europe several centuries ago, witches were said to give anyone who angered them the evil eye. They also supposedly used it to bewitch judges so they would not be convicted of witchcraft charges. Judges took care not to look accused witches in the eye, and to keep crucifixes, blessed salt and holy water handy to repel any evil vibes.

Deliberate overlooking can be deadly, but according to lore, most evil eye acts are done unwittingly by people who are unlucky enough to be born with supernatural killer looks. Such people don't mean to harm anyone, but if they look at someone or their possessions with anger or envy, or perhaps even too much admiration, the mysterious energy that emanates from their eyes can have a disastrous effect.

Most dangerous are strangers who look too long, even in

an admiring way, at people, children, animals and even posses-sions. Unless immediate action is taken, the children get sick, the animals die, the possessions are stolen, or good fortune in business turns sour.

Even high-ranking noblemen and clergy have been said to possess the evil eye. Pope Pius IX (1792-1878) was branded by his enemies as having an evil eye shortly after his investiture as Pope in 1869. While traveling through Rome in an open vehi-cle, he glanced at a nurse holding a child in an open window. Minutes later, the child fell to its death. From then on, it seemed that everything the Pope blessed resulted in disaster. Pope Leo XIII (1810-1903) was also said to possess the *mal occhio or jettatura*, as the evil eye is called in Italian, because of the number of cardinals who died while he was in office.

Defense against the evil eye

What can you do to deflect the evil eye? The ancient Egyptians protected their possessions, dwellings and tombs against the evil eye with a stylized eye amulet called the *udjatti*, also called the "Two Eyes" or the "Eye of the Sun and the Eye of the Moon." The *udjatti* were worn and painted on objects, coffins and structures. The protective eyes reflected the evil eye stare away. Sometimes a single *udjat* – also called the Eye of Horus — was used, but the amulet was most powerful if both eyes reflected the baleful glance of evildoers.

Grotesque heads of demons or monsters, such as the snake-haired Medusa of Greek mythology, also repel the evil eye.

The best defense against the evil eye is an amulet worn on the body, for a person never knows when overlooking will strike. Frogs, horns and phallus shapes are the best. Amulets can be formed with the hands in a variety of postures. A common posture is the "fig," a clenched fist with thumb thrust between the index and middle fingers, which also suggests a phallus. The custom of the phallus dates to the ancient Romans, who called upon their phallic god, Priapus, to protect them against witchcraft, bad luck and evil.

A common European amulet is a bracelet of eyes made from multi-colored beads of glass. The eyes resemble round fish eyes.

Red yarn and ribbons tied, sewn or pinned to clothing are other well-used amulets. Red is considered a color that repels evil. Blue is also effective, especially in the Middle East, where blue eyes are hung on windows and over doorways, and worn on the body in jewelry. In parts of the United States, such as the Appalachian and Ozark mountain areas, "haint blue" is a sky blue color used to paint thresholds, bedrooms, and any place where protection is needed, to keep the "haints," or spirits and ghosts, away. Haint blue also reflects the evil eye.

Among other defenses are shamrocks and garlic. Spitting also works, according to lore.

Once the evil eye strikes, can its effect be broken? According to tradition, the victim must turn to an adept — such as an older woman in the family — who has magical powers and knows a secret cure. If there is no one in the family, then the victim must seek out the services of a witch or sorcerer who can break the bad spell.

There are many magical cures for the evil eye. They usually involve reciting secret incantations, which typically are passed on from mother to daughter down family lines. An Italian remedy calls for diagnosing the evil eye and curing it with a bowl of water, olive oil, and, occasionally, salt. A few drops of oil are added to the water, which is sometimes salted. The oil may scatter, form blobs, or sink to the bottom. These formations are interpreted to determine the source of the attack. More oil is added into the water while incantations are recited, and the sign of the cross is made on the forehead of the victim. If that fails, the victim is sent to a witch for further treatment.

And finally, here is another bit of evil eye lore, about peacock feathers. Do you have any in your house? If so, you may want to get rid of them, despite their exotic beauty. A widespread belief about peacock tail feathers associates the eye in the feathers with the evil eye.

14

Moon Madness:
Fact or Lunacy?

Madness, bad luck, crime, misfortune, even pregnancy —
these ills are the fault of the full moon. Or so people have
believed ever since the first human beings looked up into the
night sky and wondered about the silvery disk of Earth's lunar
companion.

Experiences over many centuries have led people to con-
clude that the moon has a mysterious power. More superstitions exist about the moon than anything else — especially the
belief that the full moon makes people go insane. In fact, the
terms "lunatic" and "loony" come from *luna*, the Latin term
for moon. Is there any truth to the madness? Or are the superstitions insane themselves? The beliefs are so strong that at one

time they even affected the law.

Many early moon superstitions warned of the mentally disruptive dangers of moonlight. Pregnant women were told that if they went out when the moon was full they would give birth to lunatics. Passages in the Talmud and Old and New Testaments attribute lunacy to the effects of the moon.

According to lore, sleeping in the light of the moon causes madness. An old Irish superstition, holds that sleeping with the moon shining on your face produces a form of blindness and a state of idiocy called "moonstruck."

Early medicine helped forge the first supposed physiological links between the moon and insanity. Roman physicians advanced the notion that the moonlight increased moisture in the air, causing brain seizures. The sixteenth-century physician, Paracelsus, said that the moon had the "power to tear reason out of man's head by depriving him of humors and cerebral virtues." The moon, he added, was at its most powerful influence when it was full.

Links between moon and madness took root in English law. Sir William Hale, who later became Chief Justice of England, wrote in the 1600s, "The moon hath a great influence in all diseases of the brain... especially dementia; such persons commonly in the full and change of the moon, especially about the equinoxes and summer solstice, are usually at the height of their distemper."

Moon madness became accepted as fact. Dr. Benjamin Rush, one of the signers of the Declaration of Independence, wrote that "the moon, when full increases the rarity of air and the quantity of light, each of which acts upon people with various diseases, and among others, in madness." An 1827 encyclopedia stated, "When the moon is on the full, or new, people are more irritable than at other times… Insanity at these times has its worst paroxysms."

Some modern scientists have tried to validate the "lunar effect" but have come up short of scientific proof. Some have looked at the gravitational pull of the moon that affects tides and the moisture of nature. Could this effect influence chemicals and hormones in the brain to cause imbalances? No evidence is conclusive.

Yet many professionals who work in health care and law enforcement attest that on nights of the full moon, there are more accidents, violence, suicides, fires, crime and other strange behavior. It seems the moon's effect defies a scientific explanation, but happens nonetheless.

And what about those werewolves — people who transform into rampaging wolves on full moon nights? The link to the moon is more fiction than folklore fact, probably due to the associations of coyotes, wolves and dogs howling at the moon. Not every werewolf described in accounts of old required a full moon to make the transformation from human to beast.

Paranormal investigators have noticed a lunar effect in the level of supernatural activity. The night before and after a full moon are often intense. Oddly, the actual full moon night is sometimes flat. Increased activity includes haunting phenomena (spirit voices, poltergeist disturbances, apparitions) and the appearances of mysterious creatures, UFOs, and mystery lights.

We may never have a scientific explanation for "moon madness," but centuries of evidence speak a clear message. The moon rules the night, the shadows and the unknown, and the murky territory between dimensions.

15

Ouija: Good or Bad?

The late demonologist Ed Warren called the Ouija board a proven "notorious passkey to terror." When it comes to the Ouija, people have similar strong opinions and emotions: *Don't touch it! Don't even go near it! You'll be possessed!*

The Ouija has its pros and cons like any paranormal tool. What it does not deserve, however, is a bashing.

Ouija is a trademarked name of a board game; the generic term is "talking board." Though marketed as a game or toy, the Ouija hails from a class of spirit communication tools that have been in use since ancient times. In recent times talking boards have been branded as a hotline to hell. After millennia of respected usage, what happened to cause this about-face?

Hello, can I speak to a spirit, please?

Attempts to communicate with the spirit world are as old as humanity. Ancient pointing and spelling devices usually were used by specially trained diviners or priests, who served as mediums between worlds.

The forerunners of today's talking boards were developed in the Spiritualism movement in the mid-nineteenth century. One was the planchette, a triangle with two wooden legs on casters and a pencil as a third leg. It was used in automatic writing.

The Ouija as we know it began in Maryland and went into production in 1890 by the Kennard Novelty Company. The company was lost in a hostile takeover, and the patent for the Ouija was then registered in the name of William Fuld in 1892. William and his brother Isaac Fuld initially were partners but soon had a falling out. William retained the rights to the Ouija, and Isaac tried unsuccessfully to compete with similar boards.

A federal court ruling in the 1920s declared the board to be a toy, and therefore taxable, and the device has been marketed as a toy ever since. The board was sold to other gaming companies, and today is owned by Hasbro.

The origin of the name "Ouija" is a bit of a mystery.

According to one story, it means "yes" in French and German – *oui* and *ja*. Another story says the name was supplied to William Fuld by spirits who communicated on the board.

From its beginning, the board had a great deal of public appeal. It looked and sounded exotic, but was simple to use. One or more persons put fingers lightly on the tear-drop-shaped pointer and then invited spirits to spell out messages by moving the pointer to letters, numbers, "yes," "no," "hello" and "goodbye."

In its early days, the Ouija was marketed as a spirit communications device that could provide a pleasant past time for couples and families. However, mediums were not necessarily pleased to see this device put in the hands of the public – not because of "demonic" fears, but because it took business out of their parlors. The Ouija zoomed in popularity after World War I, when grieving people sought to contact dead loved ones.

The Ouija gained popularity. The all-American artist Normal Rockwell even turned it into a cover for *The Saturday Evening Post* in May 1920. But along with the benign publicity came stories in the media about spirits speaking through the Ouija who told people to do bad things, including murder. Ministers denounced the board as evil. On into the decades, the Ouija seemed to follow a schizophrenic path: one as a benign toy, and one as a dangerous instrument. Given the human fascination with evil, it is not surprising that the "bad" side of the board gained more notoriety.

However, many thousands of people have quietly used the Ouija and similar talking boards without problems. Authors of significant metaphysical and literary works owe a debt to the Ouija, among them Betty White (*The Betty Book*); Pearl Curran (aka Patience Worth); Jane Roberts (*The Seth Material*); James Merrill (Pulitzer-Prize winning poet); Chelsea Quinn Yarbro (*Messages from Michael* – note, Yarbro reported on others' work with the board); and Ruth Montgomery.

The turning point

Not surprisingly, the media have played the biggest role in shaping out opinions about the Ouija. The board entered the hall of infamy with the 1973 film, *The Exorcist,* based on William Peter Blatty's hit novel about a true story of demonic possession and exorcism. The victim was a boy, but in the fictionalization of the story, becomes a girl named Regan. The Ouija board plays a role in the possession of Regan by a powerful demon, Pazuzu.

The novel was an immediate best-seller, but it was really the movie version that terrified people.

In the wake of the film, clergy once again publicly

denounced the Ouija. Ed and Lorraine Warren, lay demonologists who were gaining fame for their investigations of demonic cases, also lectured against it use – as well as against seances and "conjuring" rituals. Almost overnight, the Ouija became branded a guaranteed welcome mat to Satan.

It's a bad rap.

Good or evil?

Like any means of accessing the spirit realm, the talking board is neutral. It guarantees nothing, determines nothing, causes nothing. What comes through the board depends on the people using the board: their intentions, their thoughts, their fears, psychological issues, and, very important, contents in their subconscious. Sometimes environment is a factor, too. For example, a highly active haunted site may influence a board experience.

"The board is not evil," says Rick Fisher, founder of the Paranormal Society of Pennsylvania, and my co-author on a book about the Ouija. Fisher has collected more than forty antique talking boards for his paranormal museum. Both of us have done extensive research on talking boards. "It all comes down to the individual," Fisher says. "If you're going to commit a crime, you'll find some reason to justify it."

thoughts, intention and will. You already have these faculties, and if you are doing paranormal investigative work, you are already using them. If you put effort into honing these skills, your paranormal work will benefit.

Any device for communicating with the spirit world should be treated with respect. Here are some tips for using a talking board. Of course, you can just put it on a table and start talking, which is what most people do. These tips provide a more structured way to go about it.

If you have reservations, concerns or fears about using a talking board – don't. Your underlying emotions will interfere in the process. Here are some additional tips:

Get your own board new. Used boards, like any pre-owned object, can carry imprints of previous owners, and can even have spirits attached to them. If you buy or are given a second-hand board, clear it yourself or consult an expert who can. Quick tip on clearing: expose to sunlight, or immerse in sea salt. Mentally cleanse in spiritual light and through invoked blessings.

Be in the optimum physical, emotional and mental condition. Never use a board, or engage in any paranormal activity, when you are physically ill or fatigued, emotionally upset, or mentally stressed. States of mind and emotion become influential factors in the experience. Negative on your end draws negative on the other end.

Set a specific purpose for communication. Use intention to invite only what you seek to respond, i.e., a specific spirit, or a deceased person, or a type of spirit. Do not make open door calls such as, "Is there anybody who would like to communicate?" Stay in control and do not let communicators manipulate you or the session.

Do the dead really answer? It is the opinion of some practitioners in the magical field, that only a shell, a fragment of a once living person, will respond. However, some board users do feel they get in touch with departed people.

Invoke a circle of spiritual protection around you. This sets a sacred space for the work. Going clockwise, visualize a circle of fire or light forming around you that protects you from all unwanted influences and presences. Invoke spiritual protection to guard the boundary and instruct all unwanted presences to stay out. Do not leave the circle as long as you are in session.

Not sure what or who to invoke for spiritual protection? Pray to whom you feel a genuine spiritual connection: religious figures, angels, saints, spiritual masters.

Limit the mobility of spirits. Use visualization and will to limit the answering spirit to the board's pointer. Do not give it permission to use you or your body, or to stay in the physical space when the session is over.

Use discernment. Validate messages. Remember that many answering spirits are masqueraders and tricksters. If a spirit says it has already moved beyond the pointer, do not believe it, but mentally hold it to the pointer. Be firm about this. Spirits are very good at seizing on doubt and fear. Once you give in to doubt and fear, you've lost the upper hand.

End the session properly. Thank and instruct the summoned spirit to depart completely. Mentally remove the protective circle and thank your spiritual help.

Cleanse the space. Spirits often leave residues behind. Cleanse the space with visualization of fire and light, and/or incense, as well as invocations of blessings.

16

The Risks of Spirit Bargaining

It was a gallant gesture, but it backfired. Rob and his girlfriend Jen were new at ghost hunting, getting the hang of things. The investigations were interesting and exciting – until one night something followed Jen home and set up shop.

She saw a dark shadow figure move quickly around her apartment, especially at night. Several times she woke up to see it in her bedroom. It frightened her badly. There were also strange knocks, thumps and footsteps in the night. Once she heard the sound of breaking glass, but when she checked, nothing was amiss.

The activity increased. Rob and Jen could not make the unwelcome spirit go away. Rob decided to divert the entity's attention. He bargained with it: "If you're going to bother someone, bother me and not Jen."

His strategy worked instantly. Jen was free of the dark entity's presence, and the atmosphere in her apartment improved immediately. The entity took up residence at Rob's with the same behavior.

But after several weeks, things took a sudden downward turn. Rob, who was always in the best of health, got sick. Everyone gets a cold or the flu on occasion, but Rob's health seemed to deteriorate, as though he couldn't get well. He also started having mishaps and bad luck. He tried to send the entity away, with no success. The dark form started manifesting during the day as well as at night. Rob had difficulty sleeping, and in concentrating during the day.

By the time Rob found someone who could help him, he felt like his life had gone to pieces. The expert he found knew how to get rid of the entity and help Rob seal his energy field against repeat invasion.

The above story represents a scenario I see all too often. The characters are composites, but the circumstances are real, and I encounter them often. As more people become involved in paranormal investigations – usually without much knowledge of the supernatural – they expose themselves to unpleasant situations that can have serious consequences of spirit attachment. Ghosts and entities may not be physical, but they can cause a great deal of turmoil in the physical realm. Sometimes it is extremely difficult to end the trouble.

Pacts are for real

The history of human dealings with disembodied spirits, including records of real experiences, folklore and even spiritual teachings, is full of warnings about bargaining with spirits. The ones who like to make deals usually are of a negative and trickster nature. No matter how good the deal sounds, there will be nothing good in it for you in the long run, unless you are exceptionally skilled and know exactly what you are doing.

Pacts and deals with spirits are real, not just the stuff of religious lessons and horror films. As far as the entities are concerned, a deal is a deal – as binding as a legal contract between human beings. If you decide you want out, too bad.

The demonic pact is one of the oldest bargains on record in supernatural lore. In exchange for whatever one desires, a demon or the Devil collects the soul at the end of the deal – usually when the person dies. In Christianity, accounts of demon pacts date to the second century CE.

Different versions of the demonic pact are told. In some, such as the story of Dr. Faust, there is no wiggling out of the bargain. After a lifetime of favors such as superior knowledge, supernatural powers, and sex with beautiful women, Faust has to pay up and spend eternity in hell.

In other versions, there is a hope of redemption. A female version of the story of Faust is Mary of Nemmegen, a six-teenth-century fictional story of a young woman seduced by the Devil. She falls as badly as Faust, and regrets it as much as he does. She appeals to the Virgin Mary, who saves her bacon. The story is a moral lesson about the consequences of sin, and how to stage a course correction.

If the entity in a pact is a Djinn, there is no getting out of the deal. Djinn are often called demons, but they are not the same. They originated in pre-Islamic Arabian lore, and they were the original inhabitants of earth, losing out to humanity. Some of them want the world back, and act out against humans. They masquerade as other entities, and harass people in the same manner as demons. Some like to collect souls, some vampirize the life force, some want service and sex, some want better access to this dimension, and some just like to make trouble for the sake of it.

Like demons, Djinn will grant your wishes – a degraded version of them exists as the genie in a bottle or lamp in folk tales. They will find a way to twist your wishes into something bad, and then they will take what is theirs in the deal – at your expense.

Demon or Djinn, whatever you ask for will not be delivered in quite the manner you expect. There is always a nasty hook.

Sometimes bargaining is necessary to remedy an issue with the Djinn. Other tactics may be necessary as well. The entire matter should be handled only by a person who is experienced in dealing with them.

At the very least, bargaining with spirits can lead to a host of rapidly escalating problems. Bargaining gives an entity "rights" to you, and powerful entities immediately latch on very tightly in a "gotcha." It is much harder to get rid of entities that attach through deals than ones who just seize an opportunity to hitchhike home with you from an active site.

How pacts are made

Supernatural literature is full of accounts of grand and formal pacts that include solemn oaths and writing in a black book in your own blood. And, magical lore is full of ways to quickly achieve ambitions and goals by following the left-hand path, a shortcut that involves conjuring and bargaining with negative entities.

In fact, pacts can be made much more informally, and sometimes without even realizing it. Deciding to serve a certain path in exchange for something you want is one way. Making promises or offers is another. Never offer an entity, "If you do_____, then I will_____."

Extreme provocation in paranormal investigation – challenging or taunting an entity to make itself known or do something dramatic — is a regrettable but growing trend, and it is easy to slip into deal-making language while engaging in it. The "unreality" paranormal investigation shows on television have popularized this outright stupid practice. The shows make the investigators look brave and adventurous, but taunting and cajoling are nothing but foolish with real and serious consequences.

Remedies

The attachments formed by bargains, pacts and deals are harder to break than attachments formed by being vulnerable in the wrong place. The first is by invitation and promise, the second is by circumstantial opportunism. Traditional methods of dislodging and banishing unwanted entities may not be sufficient for a pact attachment. Victims should nonetheless consult exorcists or spirit releasers, engage in prayers to spiritual allies, and cleanse the environment with sage, salt and water. Salt scrubs are good for the body, and salt washes made with purified water or holy water can be applied around doors. In addition, salt can be sprinkled around the perimeter of a house. None of these actions will be very effective, however, if the victim's inner defenses are weak.

There is still the matter of compensating the broken deal. Some entities will not go quietly away, but will seek a substitute payoff. They may siphon off a bit of life force or orchestrate some bad luck. They may even look for a vulnerable substitute victim.

After breaking a deal, it may also be advisable to drop paranormal or occult activities for a time. Involvement in paranormal work keeps the psychic centers open – yes, even if you think you are not psychic. Withdrawing from activity shuts off a pipeline of access and energy needed by entities to stay active in the physical realm.

Outcomes

Whether or not a deal can be broken depends on a variety of factors in each case. Entities who attach through bargains sometimes seem to go away, but they do not go permanently. Instead, they become dormant, and at some future time become active again. Entities can be dormant for years and then kick back into gear.

Sometimes entities will attach through a deal, but not act on it for a long time. The person may think they avoided trouble or got away free, when in fact they did not.

The best way to avoid problems with entities and spirits is to become educated about the paranormal and treat everything you encounter with respect. When in doubt about anything, just say no.

17

Red Flags to Avoid
in Paranormal Investigations

Paranormal investigations are unpredictable. Even when you know the activity and history of a site, you never know exactly what you will encounter there. Every investigator hopes to go home with compelling data — not with disappointments or problems. From my own experiences and my conversations with dozens of investigators and researchers, here are some of the "red flags" that can make or break the experience:

Red Flag #1: Extreme Provocation

Should investigators provoke ghosts and entities in order to get a reaction that produces phenomena? It's one thing to ask questions to prod, it's another to irritate and anger. Some investigators charge around a site screaming at the invisible residents to show themselves so that they can capture visual and audio data. They use profanity and taunts such as, "Is that the best you can do? Come on, come on and get me!"

Sometimes extreme provocation seems to get results, such as bangs and shoves — although it is uncertain whether the reactions come from entities or from a buildup of human psychokinetic energy generated and projected by the investigators themselves. In the case of "reality" shows, reactions are likely to be staged.

But are bangs and shoves really the point of an investigation? Or are they merely entertainment? An investigation looks for evidence and information related to haunting — the how and why. Getting an angry response does little to advance our understanding of the nature of hauntings, especially considering that the response may be human-generated PK.

Investigators should remember that respect for the dead is a universal belief held by human beings since ancient times. The ghosts of the dead should receive consideration. Would you barge into the home of living people and insult them? Would you drop by for a visit and demand, "Are you angry we are here?" Similar courtesy should be extended at haunted sites, and include unknown spirits and entities as well as the dead. After more than a century of organized research into apparitions and hauntings, we still have little understanding of ghosts, who the spirits are that we deal with, and why places are haunted. Most paranormal investigators have even less understanding of entities; those kinds of spirit dealings have been confined largely to magical practices in the past. The objective of investigations should be to further knowledge — not to dine out on a bruise.

Red Flag #2: Ouija boards

I have been vocal many times in *defense* of the Ouija board as an interface for spirit communication. I haven't changed my mind — I consider the Ouija and other talking boards to be neutral tools. Results obtained with them are determined by the users, places and circumstances.

However, I do not advocate using Ouija boards in investigations. Not because of the boards, but because of the *people* using them. Too often, boards are used by thrill seekers who do not take proper precautions and throw themselves wide open psychically to anything.

Also, people bring a lot of baggage to the Ouija. Many people have been conditioned by Hollywood to think that boards are evil, and thus will automatically invite trouble. These feelings lie beneath the surface and can influence what happens when a board is brought into a haunted environment. Results are often problematic.

Red Flag #3: Out of Control

I have lost track of the number of times I have heard someone in an investigation group say, "A psychic told me that I'm very psychic myself, and I have a lot of weird things happen to me — but I don't know how to control my ability."

People who are out of control in this way, and especially those who admit it, should be gently told that they would be wise to avoid investigations until they learn how to manage themselves. They are loose cannons and are at risk for getting into trouble. Maybe they like the drama. Usually they are overwhelmed with "bad vibes," or they feel they are physically attacked, usually by choking. The choking sensation may actually be a physiological throat tightening response to their fear. People who are not in control are frightened, and the throat constricts in the face of fear.

Please note, I am not saying that anyone who experiences unpleasant sensations in an investigation is out of control. Negative physical effects do happen. A person who is in control can have the experience, acknowledge it, and deflect it. Sometimes I am bombarded with quite a bit at a haunted site, and the sensations are part of a broader gathering of soft data.

Out of control people, however, are at the mercy of the environment, allowing themselves to be overcome physically and psychologically. At the very least, out of control people are distractions, forcing investigators to shift their attention away from the investigation to deal with their problems. Sometimes adverse effects continue at home, creating a whole new set of problems.

How can people learn to be in control? By taking lessons in psychic or intuition development and protection, or even energy healing. Yes, energy healing training is one of the best ways to learn how to open up, assess psychic information, and shut down safely. Every community has metaphysical people who teach these skills — and, there are plenty of self-help books available.

Red Flag #4: Hitchhikers

It happens more often than it should — something follows an investigator home, burrows in, and creates disturbances. Sometimes they lose steam and go away of their own accord — and sometimes they move in for the long haul. Getting rid of them can be difficult.

It's hard to say exactly why some entities attach themselves to people. It may have to do with a person's energy field and openness, or some unknown factors of vulnerability. The living can act like flames to moths, drawing entities who want the energy from a living person's vitality and life force. Sometimes the entities are able to latch on like leeches.

The risk of hitchhikers can be minimized by precautions. There are various techniques of visualization, breathing and prayer for bolstering a shield of protection around the aura, so that one's body, mind, and spirit are sealed from invasion. Likewise, at the end of an investigation, those techniques are employed again, and forceful instructions should be given to all entities to stay in their place and not attach and follow.

Here is one technique that I use. I visualize a secure envelope of white light around me. I visualize light coming into me through the top of my head on the intake of breath, and flowing out through the soles of my feet on the exhale. This helps grounding. I invoke spiritual protection for my body, mind, spirit, thoughts, emotions and dreams, that nothing negative or unwanted shall interfere with, influence, or attach to me. At the end of an investigation, I go through the procedure again, and shut down by visualizing blinds being drawn around me.

Sometimes hitchhikers latch on to people, anyway, despite precautions. If you feel something has followed you home, take immediate steps to order it out, and do a cleansing of your premises with prayer, lit candles and incense (and holy water if desired). Do not hesitate to get help from a third party if necessary. The longer you let something stay, the harder it will be to dislodge it.

18

Psychic Protection in Paranormal Investigations

Paranormal work has its hazards. Frequent exposure to phenomena, ghosts and entities has potential repercussions of physical and psychological stress, entity attachment and energy drains. Occasionally, even a single visit to an intensely active site has side effects. Sometimes you don't realize how much you're affected until you've gone home. Don't wait until you have a problem – you can prevent negative after-effects with a few simple precautions.

First, let's take a look at some of the negative things that can happen during paranormal investigation. Small-scale physical effects include pinches, pokes, and pushes. Those are not unusual in active sites, and they seldom have lasting effects. More serious are bruises, cuts, and choking sensations. Later on may come headaches, fatigue, body pain, nausea, dizziness, feelings of unease, and ugly mental imagery, especially when you try to go to sleep. Once you get to sleep, you may have unpleasant dreams filled with violent imagery. If something has followed you home, you may experience apparitions, shadowy figures, and poltergeist phenomena.

How likely are these effects? Most people have auras that are adequate barriers against paranormal invasion, and the average ghost hunt is not going to produce anything seriously adverse. Human beings have a long history of dealing with the unseen realms, and have developed natural and deliberate ways to keep ghosts and entities in their place.

However, paranormal investigation opens people up and increases vulnerability. Psychic sensitivity naturally increases on an investigation, even if you are not aware of it. Increased sensitivity to the environment opens up the aura. Invasion happens when something is able to get through or attach to the aura.

Here are some of the steps you can take to make sure you have a solid buffer against negativity:

Stay in good physical condition

Think twice about investigating if you feel low, ill, exceptionally tired, or depressed. Your mental and physical energy should be high and resilient. If your energy flags during an investigation, or you feel uneasy or "bad," it is a good idea to excuse yourself.

Avoid alcohol and recreational drugs

Recreational substances can interfere with your judgment and also raise your vulnerability to invasion. Occult lore holds that low-level entities are attracted to alcohol and drug effects, and I've seen evidence in support of that.

Also, be aware that some prescription medication that affects mood and energy may also affect your ability to investigate.

Start the investigation with an invocation for spiritual protection

Say a prayer or mantra, evoke the presence of spiritual guardians, make contact with an amulet such as a saint's medallion, crystal, charm, or other charged or blessed object. You don't need to be public about it. Some groups like to join in a circle and spiritual protection. There is no prayer or invocation that universally works better than another. A prayer that is heartfelt and meaningful to you will work the best.

Use the breath to buffer and release

Breathwork and visualization can strengthen your aura, and also release any negative energy you feel building up. Breathe in and visualize white light pouring through the body and radiating out into a bubble or shield all around you. Allow the light to come in through the top of your head and flow out through the feet, which will help you to stay grounded. The light shield can be augmented with mirrors to reflect negativity, or even spikes to repel negativity.

To release unpleasant physical and mental effects, imagine them flushing downward in a wash of light through the soles of the feet and into the healing earth.

Stay grounded

Pay attention to physical and mental cues concerning your comfort level. To ground yourself, place the palms of your hands flat on something solid, like a wall or table. This is a technique used by many energy healers after they have been working in altered states of consciousness. Shaking the hands to release energy also helps.

Use amulets

An amulet is an object that affords spiritual and psychic protection. Amulets have been in use since ancient times. Do they really work? Can an object, such as a stone or sacred symbol, carry power that repels negativity?

Amulets represent sources of spiritual power, and foster a sense of connection to that power. You carry that connection within you, and technically do not need the amulets themselves. However, amulets are an effective way to remind yourself of that spiritual connection.

Religious symbols are amulets, as are a variety of esoteric symbols. Stones and crystals are associated with protective properties. For example, black stones such as jet, onyx, agate, hematite and obsidian absorb and repel negative energy. Red stones, such as jasper, garnet, ruby and carnelian, are grounding and vitalizing. Amethyst enhances psychic and spiritual sensitivity. You can study the lore of stones and crystals to learn more about them.

If you don't have amulets, or forget them, are you unprotected without them? Remember, your spiritual source is always present, and your connection to it lies within. Personally, I like to carry and wear amulets, and have done so for years.

Make use of water

When you get home, take a bath or shower with sea salt. Running water helps to cleanse the aura as well as the body. In esoteric lore, both water and salt pure and will take away the negative.

If phenomena on site were strongly negative, reinforce yourself with prayer and visualization.

Establish a long-term spiritual practice

Daily meditation and prayer, even for a few minutes, will strengthen your aura and protection significantly. I've been doing both for years, and protection is second nature to me. It is in place all the time.

Body work, such as energy healing, massage, acupuncture, and medical Qi Gong also will help you stay balanced and centered. Medical Qi Gong is performed by a doctor of Oriental Medicine (OMD) and involves manipulation of your energy field to increase protection and vitality.

Paranormal investigation and research have a spiritual side. The deeper you go, the more you encounter spiritual questions and matters. Being grounded in the spiritual side not only improves your buffer, but helps you understand more about the phenomena you investigate.

If problems persist after exposure to negative phenomena, consult an expert, such as an energy healer, psychic or medium, or person experienced in dealing with spirit attachments.

19

Men in Black

Seeing a UFO or having an encounter with an alien being may seem exotic and even exciting, but some individuals who have had such experiences wish they had never happened. The reason: frightening visits from threatening men called the Men In Black. They are not the funny guys portrayed by Tommy Lee Jones and Will Smith in the *Men In Black* films. In fact, victims who have been targeted by MIB say they are no laughing matter at all.

The MIB, so named because they are literally dressed in black suits and sometimes black hats, show up without warning after a person has had an ET or UFO or missing time "incident," and warn them not to talk about it. They know where witnesses live and work, and have the unnerving ability to appear suddenly and disappear just as suddenly. They have threatened and harassed individuals and their families. They stalk people, sit in black cars outside their homes, and create telephone disturbances and even poltergeist effects. They are capable of creating severe psychological distress.

MIB apparently have been active in America since 1947, when the first "flying saucers" reports were made. They have appeared all over the world, however, and are especially active during periods of great UFO activity called flaps.

One of the earliest documented and most extreme cases of MIB occurred in 1953. The victim was Albert K. Bender, a Bridgeport, Connecticut factory clerk and enthusiast of UFOs, the occult, black magic, monsters and science fiction and horror films. Bender organized the International Flying Saucer Bureau, and through his research believed he discovered where extraterrestials come from and why they visit Earth. He wrote a letter about this to a friend, and intended to publish his findings in his bureau's magazine.

After he mailed the letter, three men dressed in black suits visited him at home. One had his letter. They told him to stop publishing information on flying saucers, and they terrified Bender so badly that he did as instructed. Following their visit, Bender was unable to eat for two days, and then became progressively ill. He admitted he had been scared to death by his sinister visitors. He acted "lobotomized," in the words of one of his friends, and suffered severe headaches, which he said were controlled by "them." If he thought about revealing his information, he was hit with a debilitating headache. He dropped all of his UFO-related pursuits.

Bender's story was featured in one of the earliest books on MIB, *They Knew Too Much About Flying Saucers*, by Gray Barker. Barker, of Clarksburg, West Virginia, was well-known as a ufologist and researcher of unusual phenomena, such as the famous Mothman case in Pt. Pleasant, West Virginia in 1966-67.

Meanwhile, Bender seemed to go round the bend. Nine or ten years after his warning from the MIB, he published a book (through Barker) called *Flying Saucers and the Three Men*. He said the MIB who had visited him were really monsters from the planet Kazik. To some, the book read like a disjointed science fiction novel.

Since then, many reports of MIB have been collected from all over the world. Whoever or whatever they are, the MIB do zero in on witnesses to alien phenomena

Characteristics

Are they humans – or aliens themselves? At first glance, the MIB look like "G-men," officials from the government dressed in dark suits, ties, shoes and hats, with white shirts. Their clothing is either oddly wrinkle-free, or very wrinkled and disheveled. Sometimes something is weirdly wrong, like bizarre-looking shoes that do not seem to fit well. Some wear the Great Seal of the United States in their lapels.

They often wear black sunglasses that obscure their eyes. They usually have dark or black hair, though blond MIB have been reported. Some have unusual hair growth, as though their head has been shaved and the hair has grown back unevenly. Many of them have slightly Asian or Indian facial features and complexions.

They drive about in large, dark or black cars, like old-style Cadillac sedans. There are either no license plates, or the plates have numbers that cannot be traced.

MIB sometimes have odd ways of walking, either as though intoxicated, or with a gliding or rocking motion as though their hips were on swivel joints. The voices of MIB also are unusual in extremes: monotones, sing-songs and whines, or sometimes eloquent in timbre.

MIB visit UFO witnesses unannounced at home or work, usually coming in twos or threes. They often pass themselves off as representatives of the federal government or military intelligence. Sometimes they appear after a sighting, but *before* the individual has contacted authorities or a UFO-related organization, thus rattling the witness that they know what happened.

Curiously, they seem to know quite a bit of personal information concerning those they visit. They use intimidation, threats and harassment, telling witnesses that they did not see what they thought they did, and they must stop their research. One UFO researcher was threatened with death by a Man In Black who claimed that a UFO abductee who died had done so because he "knew too much."

While most MIB incidents concern UFOs, they also have been reported in connection with sightings of monsters and other nonhuman entities. During the Mothman wave, a UFO flap also occurred in the mid-Ohio River Valley, and the MIB stalked witnesses of both the winged humanoid and the UFOs.

Explanations

Folklorists link the MIB to legends of the Devil, who in earlier times was often said to appear in the form of a tall black man or a man in black. MIB have also been linked to the Trickster, a cosmic force at play in the paranormal.

It seems unlikely they are agents of the aliens themselves who are trying to keep a lid on UFO research and dissemination of information. The global media on ETs and UFOs is too big to control. And, not all witnesses are targeted by MIB.

Some skeptics have suggested that Barker created the MIB as a hoax; this does not explain all the MIB reports from around the world. Other skeptics say MIB are imaginary projections of the witness's own fears. That assumes that all UFO witnesses are frightened by their experiences.

Men in Black remain a mystery. They are "ultraterrestrials," or unknown entities from a parallel realm. To MIB victims, there is nothing imaginary about them.

20

Vampire UFOs

They are not your usual UFOs — mysterious lights moving about the sky. They are "vampires in the sky," literally killer UFOs that shoot deadly beams of red light at humans and animals. Vampire UFOs may sound straight out of a B science fiction movie, but the victims who get hit by the red beams sicken and sometimes die, of bizarre wasting conditions. Victims believe their blood and life force have been mysteriously vampirized away.

Lethal UFO attacks have been reported for decades. In 1946, a man in Brazil was struck by a UFO beam of light while returning from a fishing trip. His flesh fell off his bones, and he died six hours later. His body rapidly decomposed. In 1954, UFO beams reportedly burned to death an entire village and their livestock in Nairobi, Africa one night. In 1969, a man near Anolaima, Colombia was irradiated by a UFO. He became seriously ill and blue spots appeared all over his skin. He died within a few days.

In South America, the vampire UFOs are called *chupa-chupas*, or "suck-sucks," named after the goat bloodsucker entity called the *chupacabra*. The term *chupa-chupa* is derived from *chupacabra*, or "goatsucker," a vampiric creature prominent in the folklore of Puerto Rico and Central and South Americas, and which also has been reported in the United States and elsewhere around the world. The *chupacabra* stands erect on animal hind legs, has arms ending in claws, is covered with fur, has membranes like bat wings, and glowing red eyes. It sucks the blood from farm and domestic animals, killing them. In 1996, an alleged chupacabra attack on a human was reported in Mexico. The victim, a woman, was clawed on the back. The wounds resembled burn marks. Some *chupacabra* attacks on animals have been linked to UFO sightings.

Human *chupa* victims who have survived the killer UFO attacks suffer chronic physical complaints such as weakness and dizzy spells. Some suffer mentally with fear and paranoia.

In his book *Confrontations*, Jacques Vallee documents cases of *chupa-chupas* that affected three towns in Brazil in the early 1980s: Parnama, Sao Luis and Belem. The bodies of some of the victims looked as though they had had the blood sucked out of them. The victims were either out hunting and fishing at night, or sleeping in hammocks at home. The ones who were attacked while sleeping reported that they awakened to feel hit by a heavy weight on their chest that immobilized them. One pregnant woman suffered bruising from the UFO beams, and then miscarried. A barking dog was struck by a beam, and suffered a wasting away until it died about three weeks later.

In one case, two hunters, Ribamar Ferreira and Abel Boro, were struck by a *chupa* light. According to Vallee:

It was so bright that it turned night into day... Abel screamed as the object — looking in this case like a giant spinning tire truck with lights on it — surrounded his body with a glittering glow. Ferreira ran to Abel's house and returned with his family: they found Abel Boro dead, his body white "as if drained of blood."

Vallee said that it is natural for corpses to look whitish-gray, because hemoglobin begins to break down after death. However, this does not explain the abnormally low hemoglobin found in dozens of victims who were not killed immediately by *chupas*. Vallee reported about a woman who, was struck in the chest by a beam, which left two puncture marks on her left breast. The woman had a decrease in red blood cells, and suffered dizziness, headaches, weakness, and numbness. She deteriorated, fell into a coma, and died.

Ufologist Bob Pratt documented additional cases of vampire UFOs, mostly in South America, in his book *UFO Danger Zone*. For example, from July 1977 to November 1978, a wave of deadly UFO sightings and encounters around Colares, Brazil killed people and at least one animal — a dog — and left others seriously ill. In all, about forty people, most of them adults, received medical treatment for injuries. Most of the victims were struck by mysterious beams of red light that severely burned their chests. Blood tests showed the victims to have abnormally low levels of hemoglobin. Some of the victims did not die directly from the burns, but suffered a wasting away over a period of months, and then died. Many people in the area believed that the ETs in the UFOs had come specifically to suck the blood or energy from people.

One victim, a woman, described how she was sleeping in a hammock in her house one night when she was awakened by a green light shining in her window. The beam turned to red. She saw that it came from what appeared to be a pistol wielded by something that looked like a man wearing a diving suit. She could see it only from the chest up; it had very small eyes. It pointed the pistol at her chest and shined a red beam on her three times. The beam was hot and she felt as though it took blood out of her. The beam left three pinpoint scars in a triangle just above her right breast. According to Pratt, the woman testified:

It was hot and it hurt... It was like being stuck with a needle. I bled at all three points. At the moment it happened I got very thirsty. I was terrified, but I couldn't move my legs. I was paralyzed. I was very frightened and I screamed and screamed.

The woman's screams awakened her cousin, who came to her aid. The mystery creature disappeared. The victim was taken to the hospital and treated. For weeks, she suffered a headache and fever and general malaise.

One doctor who treated victims of the UFO attacks observed that they had small puncture wounds on their arms. She thought they had had blood taken. The wounds were not similar to the bites of vampire bats.

Are vampire UFOs related to the animal mutilations associated with other UFO activity? UFOs have been linked to mysterious animal mutilations in the United States and elsewhere in the world since at least 1967, when the phenomenon gained worldwide attention with the case of the mutilated and murdered horse, Snippy, in the San Luis Valley of Colorado.

The animal mutilations often happen in waves. Hundreds of cows, sheep, dogs, horses and other animals have been completely ex-sanguinated, with tongues, eyes and vital organs removed with surgical precision. Animal predators and cruel humans are not satisfactory explanations. It is not possible to

sons who have logged in study and experience to acquire the knowledge and skills to deal with a variety of situations. Dealing with the entities who populate the multiverse requires discernment. Not everything negative is a "demon." Some problems are solved easily and some require deeper and longer remedies.

Unfortunately, many paranormal investigation groups are not educated about the paranormal beyond manipulating their equipment, and many religious personnel, including priests and ministers, are ill-equipped to deal with a genuine manifestation of an entity.

I often recommend consulting qualified individuals in the healing and shamanic arts. They have undergone instruction and training to discern and deal with the unseen environment. Depending on the nature of the problem, it may be appropriate to consult an energy healer, a past-life therapist, a practitioner of medical Qi Gong, a soul healer, a shaman, a medium, a practitioner of magic, a demonologist, or an exorcist. In terms of the latter two, demonologists and exorcists, there are many types in addition to the Catholic priests portrayed in most films.

Actually, the very best experts have knowledge touching on most of those areas just mentioned. It is not always necessary to do on-site visits for at least initial consultations, for some work can be done on a non-local basis. Some experts may prefer or even need to do on-site visits. Every situation is different, of course, and depending on the entities involved, more than one expert may need to be consulted.

In general, natural causes should be reasonably eliminated first, including environmental, physical, psychological, emotional and mental factors. Getting at the root of the problem may take some time and digging.

Personal referrals are often the best way to find the right help. Recommendations can also be obtained from staff at alternative healing centers, health food stores, and metaphysical book stores and centers. Use search engines on the Internet.

A word about fees for services: some people charge, some do not. Some may ask for reimbursement of gas and travel. Do not expect to get everything free. Some experts make their living and support their families this way, and so you pay them the same as you would a doctor, a dentist, a psychotherapist, a lawyer, or anyone else who performs a service for you. At the same time, beware of individuals and groups who charge big fees for vague services such as "clearings." Check credentials and don't be shy about asking for references. Pay attention to your own gut instinct: if something does not feel right, move on.

About the Author

Rosemary Ellen Guiley is a leading expert on paranormal and spiritual topics and is the author of more than forty-seven books and hundreds of articles on a wide range of topics. She has had a life-long interest in the paranormal, and has worked full-time in the field as a researcher, investigator and author since the early 1980s. She conducts her own original field investigations and research on negative hauntings, portals, entity contact experiences, and spirit communications.

Her books include nine single-volume encyclopedias. She does frequent media and public lecture appearances. You can find out more about her and her work on her main website, Visionary Living, at www.visionaryliving.com.